PRAISE FOR
CINCHOLOGY

"This fast-moving book is loaded with great ideas you can use immediately to improve every part of your personal and business life. Get more done, faster. Earn more money. Take complete control of your life."
— **Brian Tracy, Author, Speaker, Consultant**

"*Cinchology* is a well-defined roadmap to leading a successful life. It is written by an extraordinary man who has reached great heights on a journey that began in a childhood battered by a depth of poverty that would have permanently crippled most. I have known and admired Robert Louis Poole since he was little Bobby, the sweet child who'd just been taken from his family by child welfare. I remember him well, wearing too tight clothes and hand-me-down shoes, undaunted. Even then, he had remarkable grit, ingenuity, and determination along with uncommon gentleness and the joyful optimism that would bring his family back together, help him triumph over any and all hardships thrown his way, and ultimately make it possible for him to achieve great success in every area of his life. *Cinchology* shares with the reader his essential lesson that all good work is hard work, a guiding principle that has made him a great father and husband and successful entrepreneur. For Bobby, the keenest of listeners, giving back has always been as important as succeeding, so it is no surprise that he has taken all he has learned to teach others seeking to improve their own lives these well-earned effective step-by-step lessons. Cinchology is infused on every page with his wisdom, humility, gratitude, humor, and joy."

— Gretchen Buchenholz, Founder and Executive Director of the Association to Benefit Children and life-long friend

"Life is filled with ups and downs as well as many unexpected twists and turns. In *Cinchology*, author Robert Poole shares life lessons in a transparent and vulnerable way that go well beyond the cliché of "when life gives you lemons, make lemonade." His often-funny stories demonstrate the power of intention, grit and the resilient capacity of the indomitable human spirit! Cinchology's use of stories, examples and self-examination exercises can put a life of abundance within the reader's grasp!"

— Cindy Kent, Former, President and General Manager, 3M Infection Prevention Division

"*Cinchology* is completely absorbing and packed with one surprising breakthrough after another. This book is filled with transformation!"

— Ron Hubsher, Author of *Closing Time: The 7 Immutable Laws of Sales Negotiation*

"Insightful ideas wrapped in real-life personal stories. Robert Poole's breakthroughs and success is an inspiration to those that struggle with stress and work-life balance."

— **Scott Hogle, Senior Vice President of Sales, iHeart Media and Author of** *Persuade: The 7 Empowering Laws of the SalesMaker*

"*Cinchology* provides wonderful inspiration and tactics for living with intent. I simply loved reading it and am implementing a few new ideas."

— **Justin Tomlinson, Author of** *Live With Intent: Creating Your Future*

"I've thoroughly enjoyed reading *Cinchology*. Robert relates life stories into thought-provoking scenarios of determination and positivity making for an engaging and fun read. The theme of simplifying difficult tasks into incremental steps, done efficiently, and with care can make any task a cinch to follow. I like the short chapters focused on unique themes (especially baseball!) and the end of chapter bullets."

— **Todd Olson, Director of Sales, Greensboro Grasshoppers, Class A Affiliate of Florida Marlins**

"When life is thrown at you - point blank - and is tougher than anticipated, turn to this amazing book and apply these timeless and proven principles to change your game."

— **Thomas Reichart, Author of** *Live With Intent: Creating Your Future*

"*Cinchology* inspires and motivates the reader to challenge and engage some of life's biggest challenges. It reflects Robert Poole's resilient spirit."

— **Michael S. Salone**, CEO 3-6TY and Author of *Tagging For Talent: The Hidden Power of Social Recognition in the Workplace*

"*Cinchology* contains many nuggets of gold when it comes to understanding success mindsets. Thought-provoking, challenging, and if you apply is sure to move you forward personally and professionally."

— **Elliott Neff**, CEO of Chess4Life and Author of *A Pawn's Journey*

"*Cinchology* by Robert Poole is an easy read and well worth the time spent to make an immediate impact on your ability to achieve your personal, family and professional goals. Concise and filled with applicable examples from his personal journey which allow the reader to easily identify with and relate. Simply read on your daily commute or flight between meetings – use this book during those times to improve your ability to achieve your goals. Highly recommended."

— **Mark Fung**, RADM, CEC, USN

"Robert beautifully transcribes his personal experiences and continuous passion for family and learning into a work of art and science. Like an architect, he erects for readers a journey that raptures and bounds emotionally excerpts from an incredible life full of challenges and successes, each providing a wealth of insight. The essence of his character, core values, passion for excellence, and love for helping others are chiseled into every page. I have witnessed *Cinchology* in real-time and it resides in his heart and soul; the ultimate gem-a must read!"

— **Carlos Del Castillo**, Award-Winning
Sales and Marketing Consultant

Cinch-ology

[cinch-**ol**-*uh-jee*]

noun

1. a branch of learning for systematically seizing business
   opportunities while upholding a well-balanced home life.
   "the Cinchology process is easy to learn and highly impactful"

verb

2. informal. study to seize on or make sure of:
   "Bob's insight cinched Joe's decision to compete in a race"

CINCHOLOGY®

Achieving BIG Breakthroughs
One Inch at a Time

BY

ROBERT LOUIS POOLE

Made for Success
PUBLISHING

158.1

PUBLISHED BY MADE FOR SUCCESS PUBLISHING,
a division of Made for Success, Inc., Seattle, Washington.

If you are seeking to purchase this book in quantity for sales
promotion or corporate use, please contact Made for Success at
425-657-0300 or email Sales@MadeforSuccess.net. Your local
bookstore can also help you with discounted bulk purchase
options.

Library of Congress Cataloging-in-Publication data

Poole, Robert Louis
Cinchology™: Achieving BIG Breakthroughs
One Inch at a Time

ISBN: 978-1-64146-302-7 (PBK)
ISBN: 978-1-64146-303-4 (EBOOK)
LCCN: 2018945946

Printed in the United States of America

*This book is dedicated to my family;
my amazing wife, Maria, for supporting me
through all of my 'out of left field ideas'
and to our two wonderful
daughters, Cara & Amanda.*

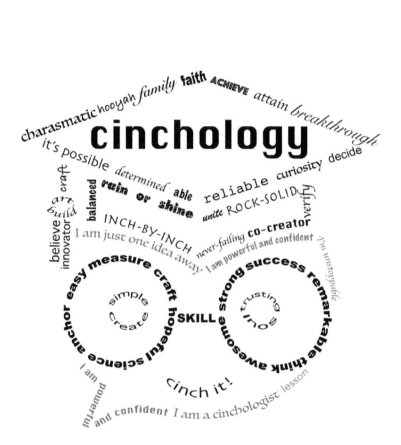

TABLE OF CONTENTS

ACKNOWLEDGMENTS

In gratitude to Jesus and my angels.

A special thank you to my family for their love, encouragement, and patience throughout the process. You really make life a cinch.

I also wish to acknowledge and thank the following people who used their skill and creativity to edit this book: My beloved daughters, Cara & Amanda for their input. Thank you for sharing your God-given talents. You both have an amazing future ahead of you.

To my pal Carlos Del Castillo, for your unbelievable friendship and acumen. You epitomize what a family man is all about. Truly inspiring!

My friend and business coach Chris Widener. You have a remarkable ability to bring out the best in people. I'll be eternally grateful.

To Bryan Heathman, DeeDee Heathman, and Katie Alspaugh at Made for Success Publishing. You folks are true professionals in every sense. Thank you for the tremendous support!

Lastly, thank you to all the unique people who gave me a chance at life and opened the door of possibility. You will always hold a place in my heart and mind. There are too many to mention here.

FOREWORD

I 've been in the personal development world for about 30 years and have traveled all over the world teaching people how to be successful in their lives and businesses. One of the things that I have always said is that success is simple. It's hard, but it's simple. As it has been said, success is just doing the right things day by day until you get there.

I love the message of my friend Robert Poole's *Cinchology*. It is the latest example of the teaching that while there is not a quick fix, one can achieve success by making small changes and moving forward one inch at a time. In the movie Any Given Sunday, Al Pacino's character, the coach of a professional football team, gives a speech toward the end of the movie wherein he forcefully makes the point that football, like life, is a game of inches. So true. Life is a game of inches. Success is a game of inches.

Ultimately that is great news for all of us because most people are afraid of moving forward because they think that they have to scale too much, too fast. But the truth is that in spite of the stories of those who rise fast, most people achieve success a little bit by little bit. Slowly moving forward in life and business is the way that usually works.

Robert helps you understand the difference between stumbling blocks and stepping stones. He not only helps you understand the difference between them, but how to leverage them. No longer will stumbling blocks stand in your way. Even troubles become stepping stones to greater success.

This book also teaches you how to set and achieve milestones. Goals are something that every successful person has. They, "begin with the end in mind" as Stephen Covey put it in his book *The Seven Habits of Highly Effective People*. And the key to achieving goals and milestones is to have absolute measurable results. If you cannot measure the results, you'll never know if you got there or not.

Robert is a big believer in family and understands that family is at the core of society. In its smallest form of community family is the bedrock for everything that matters most.

Ultimately what this book is about is success. Success with your family, your business, and your life. Success isn't the overachievement in one area, but the balanced achievement in all areas. A well-balanced life is possible while still achieving the kind of success that you hoped for.

When the tough times come, and they surely will, the difference between the successful and the unsuccessful is that the successful live life with resilience. They just simply persist in the face of trouble. The reason they can do this is because they have developed the mindset that says that they will move forward at any cost and nothing will get in their way. Even if they only move forward an inch, that's enough to move them forward, closer to their goals.

Robert has lived a very unique life and brings the stories of his life alive with rich color, helping us understand the basic principles of life and success.

Life isn't easy. If it was, everybody would win, but they don't. The people who win understand that they need to constantly be moving forward, even if it's just a little bit. That little bit becomes the platform for your next game. Read *Cinchology*. Take notes. Go back through it again. But above all, apply it. As you read through the book, be thinking of ways that these lessons apply to you. Then go apply them. The only way you achieve success in life is to actually do something. Life rewards action.

I can't help it, but every time I hear the word *Cinchology*, I think of the old quote by Robert Schuller. Inch by inch, it's a cinch. Dr. Schuller made that quote famous, and now Robert is putting even greater legs on it.

Chris Widener, author of *The Angel Inside* and *The Art of Influence*.

INTRODUCTION

"So few are the easy victories as the ultimate failures."
– **Marcel Proust**

W hy do so many people make things so complicated? Why are relationships so hard? Why do families break apart? Why is finding a good job so challenging? Why am I always falling behind? Why am I always feeling stressed? Why can't things be easier? Why, why, why? No matter where I've been or what I've done in my personal and professional life, I've frequently heard these questions muttered by people time and time again. These worries seem to affect a lot of wonderful people.

**they are signs and symptoms of _____
(fill in the blank)**

Signs are what a trained professional sees and symptoms are what a person experiences or feels. This may help avoid a potential disaster. You may have experienced this during a medical consult with a healthcare professional. Let's talk about this little-known thing called stress for a moment since it impacts a very large number of people, especially in the workplace. Although stress is a normal part of life and may serve a useful purpose, research shows that unmanaged stress is a contributing factor to cancer, heart disease, phobias, and other life-threatening consequences.[1] In fact, it's known as The Silent Killer.

A recent documentary revealed that stress shrinks your brain, adds fat to your body, and even unravels your chromosomes.[2] Some people get so comfortable with stress they just don't feel it anymore, even though the signs and symptoms are present for the world to see. This pattern is similar to a diabetic who gets so accustomed to chronic hyperglycemia or prolonged high blood sugars that they don't feel symptoms anymore; this is highly dangerous for a diabetic, and it's equally dangerous for the person who is constantly stressed.

In the pursuit of increased performance, competition and perfection, it seems stress has become the main plea for all that goes wrong in a person's life — whether it's related to family; the workplace; education; medical profession; military or money; you name it. The truth is conditions where people live and work are absolutely vital to their health. Empirically speaking, it's my belief that we not only survive longer with less stress, but we also thrive more without stress. I'm living proof of that. I've taken the CINCHOLOGY® approach to life and never let my creativity and imagination grow up and get lost. I may have suffered great loss as a child, but managed to never lose my imagination; always believing we are **C**harismatic **I**nnovators **N**ever-failing **C**o-Creators Hooyah! Hang in there with me, and you'll discover more in the following sections.

Achieving big breakthrough success and balance at work and home is both an art and science that can be obtained by following a process or prescription. From this vantage point, I've invested years studying art and design in New York City, beginning at the High School of Art & Design, Pratt Institute, Fashion Institute of Technology and Adelphi University, and completed a few years in the creative industry for a living. On the medical science and life-science side of the spectrum, I've spent the last twenty years in healthcare exploring disease states in the highly competitive medical device industry in sales, sales training, and sales management for two Fortune 500 companies, a Global 500 company, and a Global 2000 company, as well as two start-up medical device companies.

As a professional artist and a sales professional, I've learned you'll always be accepted and rejected. As an individual contributor in medical device sales, I've personally generated over 14 million dollars in sales revenue in my selling career. I'm often asked, "How did you make that career leap between art and science?" The short answer is simply by being fascinated and genuinely interested in people, paying attention to everything, being curious, satisfying natural cravings, and a strong desire to be closer to my wife, children, and family. It also helped that art and science are actually related in so many ways. It all involves observation, investigation and asking lots of good questions.

So, I thought, what would be a good way to explore more of the world? The U.S. Navy! My dad enlisted as a Merchant Marine during WWII and served in the U.S. Army during the Korean War. I reshaped my life by enlisting in the U.S. Navy, specializing in fire science and metal-working. Incidentally, humans have a lot in common with metals as it relates to strength, toughness, stress, and fatigue. Both human resilience and metals have a breaking point, so to speak. This can happen when we are under too large of a stress load, or even an accumulation of small stressors over time. How far can metal bend without breaking? The same question can apply to our lives. What bonds could be formed? The military was a terrific platform for me to stretch and discover. Damage control was a large part of this process training shipboard personnel in ship stability; fire prevention and firefighting; and chemical, biological and radiological warfare defense. I trained intensely in compartmental damage control. Each of these jobs was super competitive, high pressure and high expectation roles in which poor outcomes can be devastating.

After serving in the U.S. Navy, I volunteered as a firefighter and medic with an engine company and rescue unit on Long Island, NY. In addition, I started several small businesses: the first business was a home-safety, first-aid and CPR training company with a special emphasis on mothers with young children, youth organizations and professional first-responders; another was an e-commerce joint venture with my best friend and business partner. I've certainly experienced a tremendous number of stressful situations in all of these arenas.

Over these amazing years, I've met and worked with incredibly talented and ultra-competitive individuals, and they too had experienced difficulty managing stress between work obligations and family. Some suffered terribly physically, emotionally and financially, and so did their families. Just take a look at divorce rates these days, for example. Half of first marriages end in divorce. Second and third marriage divorce rates are even greater.[3] Regrettably, families are torn apart all too often. I know that's a major price in life to pay since being affected by loss at a young age myself.

Each of us has faced enormous challenges and barriers at different points in our lives. These pivotal experiences made me reflect a lot on my life and how I compensated for the outrageous formative years, and how it actually impacted my critical thinking and belief system.

My three main objectives are very simple:

a. to live the fullest life with family and friends
b. to live as stress-free as I can and enjoy everyday life
c. to live in abundance as nature intended and love my work

The roots of my success in these three areas are reinforced by two decades of research, including working directly with innovators, hundreds of medical professionals, and hundreds of patients related to managing disease; reading over 200 books on self-improvement and business; reviewing over a 1000 clinical articles from various professional journals; and participating in hundreds of hours of productivity, leadership and healthcare courses to design the life I wanted for myself and for my family. Additionally, I've been a valued member of advisory boards and councils within major corporations and university. I also possess an awesome library in my home. That, my friend, is what CINCHOLOGY® encapsulates. So where does this leave you and I, and why should you continue reading this book?

This book is written for anyone who has ever struggled to achieve great success in their career while balancing family and friends; for those who are facing a job transition or who have just finished college and are looking for their first real job; for those in the military, medical, teaching, arts or business professions. In short, this book is for everyone.

The goal of this book is to be both entertaining and educational. For starters, it's a wonderful, simple pleasure to curl up with a good book, especially if you are feeling stressed-out, or if you simply want to learn a proven process to get ahead a little bit easier and faster. It's like adding awesome sauce to your diet.

Research shows that reading has short-term and long-term effects on connecting in the brain and is one of the most effective ways to overcome stress. Emory University conducted a clinical research project to show how stories get into your brain.[4,5] Previous research conducted at the University of Sussex[6] suggests that reading a good book is more effective than listening to music (which I love both), going for a walk or drinking tea (again, things I love to do... actually, I enjoy drinking kaw-fee as we would say in Yorkville NYC).

Although I may not know who you are personally, chances are there may be an opportunity for you to gain insight from the CINCHOLOGY® process. After all, it's measured changes that lead toward results.

Meeting new people, learning new things and sharing ideas is an absolute joy for me, which I treasure, and I'm sharing that insight with you here. This book is designed to be read from beginning to end since I will be going back and forth, from present to past. However, there is no right or wrong way to read this book. It's packed with useful information to help you excel in business and home.

My recommendation for you would be to have a pen or pencil handy for taking notes as you read, as your own ideas will begin to flow like a river. A Chinese Proverb says the palest ink is better than the best memory. I couldn't agree more! I'm well known for taking effective notes, and so are my daughters. It's the first Cinch It tip.

Take effective notes

Believe me when I say taking good notes is a rare skill these days. Sadly, it's even rarer for someone to review what they've written even once, let alone regularly. Not taking good notes — or not taking notes at all — deprives us of the opportunity to take stock. What a shame that would be. I'll be sharing tried-and-tested tips with you throughout this book, so feel free to write in your own book or on a handy-dandy CINCHOLOGY® notebook.

If you are a digital person, I still recommend handwritten notes over digital. You can always transfer your ideas later. There are actually many places in our society where you are not permitted to use a digital device, but having your trusted book and pen is A-Okay! There are blank pages available in this book to capture ideas as we go. After all, most of us only get one shot at life, so let's make the rest of our life, the best of our life.

You can make it any distance beginning inch-by-inch.

You are only one simple idea away.

This is going to be special! Ready, set, let's go!

Hooyah!

SECTION ONE:
INNER CHILD AND NEW BEGINNINGS

CINCH IT #1

FIREPROOF

"Sometimes God will deliver you from the fire,
and other times God will make you fireproof."
– Joel Osteen

" BOBBY, don't lean out of the window like that, you
can slip!" Mom shouted from inside the apartment.

"Sorry, Mommy," I replied while leaning back in her
bedroom window.

As I looked outside my top floor apartment window to
draw some pictures of the city, I saw High Bridge Park and
Water Tower in view near New York City's forgotten bridge.
Manhattan is full of changing shapes. Suddenly, a loud
noise and orange light caught my attention as the sound
of broken glass echoed across the roof of an apartment

building on 173rd Street between Saint Nicholas Avenue and Audubon Avenue. As I saw flames and black smoke billowing through the window on the top floor, I was filled with fear. The flames were only visible from my vantage point; hidden from the street. While pointing to the smoke, I began shouting "FIRE! FIRE! FIRE!" to get the family's attention below on the street. "Bobby, what in the world are you...?" Mommy responded as she ran toward the window and noticed the fire I was pointing at. "Oh my goodness, oh no!!" she gasped. My younger brother Jimmy shouted "FIRE! FIRE! FIRE!" until the family downstairs heard our calls for help. We didn't have a telephone in the apartment.

"Mommy! I can feel the fire!" I said.

Moments later, I recall hearing the distinctive, powerful horns and sirens from the fire trucks wailing down the avenue, consuming the neighborhood. It was the first time I felt the sensation of fear; blood flowing through my body, causing my heart to pound in my skinny eight-year- old frame. I sat there and watched the firemen gather their tools and orchestrated a plan of attack and rescue. A smaller FDNY truck turned the corner. Two men got out of it and set up a poster board on the hood. The family on the street walked over to them and pointed up towards the window, and they both looked up at us. We stayed by the window, marveling at the firefighters working their magic.

A few weeks had passed since the fire, and the air was still tainted by the badly charred material. Smoke damage leaves a smell that is difficult to remove. We kept our windows in the apartment shut because of it.

"KNOCK, KNOCK, KNOCK."

"Mommy, someone's at the door," I said. "Who is it?" she called out.

"It's the Fire Department," a voice is heard behind the door.

Mommy looked through the peephole and saw two firemen dressed in uniform. She opened the door and greeted them with "Hello, how are you?"

"Are you Mrs. Poole, ma'am?" the senior fireman asked. "Yes, how may I help you?" Mommy responded.

"You were at the fire!" I said, pointing excitedly. "That's right, son, we were there," the senior fireman said.

"We would like to commend your boys for discovering the fire," the senior fireman said with a hoarse, raspy voice as if he smoked a lot. The junior fireman held out a package and said: "thank you for the quick response; you boys saved people." They reached out and shook our hands with authority, and the junior fireman said, "on behalf of the FDNY, thank you," and disappeared as their walkie-talkies sounded off.

Mommy removed the plaque, and I noticed something wasn't right by the expression on her face.

"That was thoughtful of them to share this," Mommy says.

"Can I see, Mommy?" I asked.

"For some reason, your name is not on here," she said as she handed it to me. The plaque only had my brothers' names on it.

"That's not fair. I saw it first," I said.

Mommy paused for a brief moment, then looked me in the eyes and said, "Robert Louis Poole! Mistakes happen. Life isn't always fair. Always be grateful for what you have." When your mommy calls you by your full name, you better listen. I've learned to be extraordinarily grateful for everything. The point here is that it's impossible to be dissatisfied and appreciative at the same time. An attitude of gratitude guides a verve of expectancy in our devotions.

Since childhood, I've been fascinated with the notion of the gift of serving people, especially from the viewpoint of a New York City Firefighter. My brothers and I learned the consequences of fire play when one day we unintentionally set our own bedroom curtains on fire while tossing lit paper airplanes near the window. We pretended to be a gutsy Marine attack pilot from the Baa Baa Black Sheep Squadron. We were able to craft awesome paper airplanes that glided the air like a bird drifting in a summer breeze. After that incident, we never started another fire. I was shocked to watch how badly something can get out of control so fast and learned some valuable life lessons such as the law of unintended consequences. The firefighters worked behind the scenes to fulfill God's work. That day, they not only saved us, but educated me in more ways than I could ever learn on my own.

As a young kid, I began visiting local fire stations, including NYFD's Marine 1 located at Battery Park. There's a well-known fireboat called Fire Fighter that served the City for over 70 years. In fact, it was put on display at the 1939 World's Fair in New York City and served alongside other NYFD Marine Units as the source of water for firefighter efforts at Ground Zero in 2001. Watching boats and ships travel up and down the Hudson, Harlem and East Rivers also captivated me. The Port of New York and New Jersey is one of the busiest ports in the United States, if not the world. It was natural for me to be thinking of joining the U.S. Navy at a young age since I wanted to "see the sea and seek." By the way, notice it doesn't take much to change the meaning of a word by simply replacing or adding a letter. Kind of like life. One simple change can make the difference.

preparation meets opportunity

Prior to deployments, the U.S. Navy and U.S. Coast Guard conduct many evaluations of an At-Sea Fire Party aboard ships. The Damage Control team are the rapid response members aboard Naval ships, similar to the fire department in any city or town. As I turned twenty years old, I was proud to become the On-Scene Leader for the At-Sea Fire Party, as well as the Repair Locker 5 for General Quarters Stations. An LST is a version of a Tank Landing Ship of World War II. The On-Scene Leader in Repair Locker 5 leads the team's damage control efforts in the main propulsion spaces. The role is usually reserved for veteran sailors because it requires tremendous skillsets and know-how, and you are responsible for the team's lives.

This was a dream role for me, and I really wanted it, so I studied every aspect of the job, including mastering every assignment leading up to it, and competed smartly for it. As new sailors came aboard, I took the initiative to properly train them on their required Personal Qualification Standards for basic Damage Control — survival at sea. PQS is a compilation of the minimum knowledge and skills a sailor must demonstrate for damage control readiness despite their primary job. Some trainers would simply present verbally and sign off on it. Not me. I took advantage of multiple layers of learning styles. Most people have a combination of learning styles and don't fit under a particular one — more importantly, we must apply the content, not just the study:

a. visual learner – learn best through seeing; enjoying pictures, diagrams and visuals; videos are a great tool.

b. kinesthetic learner – best matched for physical activity and participation; love use of hands; their recall is also higher with activities they've participated in prior.

c. auditory learner – intense listeners and have terrific memories; prefer oral presentations over writing reports.

I have found that it's very powerful to assess a person's dominant learning style to create an excellent communication plan. Each person's learning style is unique. To assist in understanding, I would ask Socratic questions that caused people to think throughout the process, and followed up with additional questions to create more engagement and establish trust (e.g., "Why did you join the Navy?" "How did you choose your rate?" and "What's your expectation with this training?"). One-by-one, I kept training the sailors on the aspects of basic damage control. By doing so, I amped up my knowledge and skillsets tenfold because I was getting a great deal of extra practice above and beyond the routine drills we would have. I also felt safer going out to sea with my shipmates. In fact, as new sailors reported to the ship, I was sought after to train them. That made me very visible for new opportunities.

This process also served me well while my command was on a deployment in West Africa. We were part of an amphibious task and landing force also known as the Gator Navy. We were trained, organized and equipped to perform amphibious operations along with the U.S. Marines. While at sea with other ships, we would compete in our version of the Olympics called Damage Control Olympics. The best damage control crew were selected from each ship to form a team and then compete in various damage control evolutions against each command. The "DC Games" were held on the larger LHA or LHD class ships, since they are small aircraft carriers — lots of room to play on their flight decks. It was exhilarating for us to win the coveted Gold Spanner Wrench and display it onboard! We were flawless because we made our mistakes in training and practice, not where the "fit hits the shan."

The At-Sea Fire Party practices how to deal with various types of fires that occur at sea, and every facet of the process is measured and judged. Measuring is an important part of any endeavor. What gets measured gets done. It's pretty simplistic to measure inch-by-inch steps. This same principle applies to our own lives. For example, a business may measure a salesperson's success in daily, weekly, monthly sales revenue and rankings compared to his or her peers. It could also be measured in the value they bring to a person or group. It's about establishing intended results and defining what success looks like beforehand.

There are approximately eighteen members with specific roles on the At-Sea Fire Party team with three main objectives:

    a.   respond immediately to fire alarms and measure everything

b. extinguish fires effectively without disrupting operations

c. control fires until ongoing critical evolutions can be concluded and General Quarters Stations (GQ) are ready.

"Ding-ding-ding... This is a drill! This is a drill! Fire! Fire! Fire! Class Bravo fire in Main Engine Room..." the announcement came over the 1MC general announcing system in the middle of the night, waking the sleeping crew. Variability is important in any training. Anything can happen at any time, in port or out at sea.

I leapt out of my rack from a sound sleep; reflex kicked in as I ran, donned my gear and quickly got on the scene while two shipmates were evacuating the main engine room where the call for action was made. "Tell me what you've got, Chief," I said.

"Had an explosion and spray fire in the hydraulic system piping and it spread to the bilge. Two casualties down, forward and starboard-side," the Chief rapidly reported.

I quickly captured the details and relayed the information to the Repair Party Leader located in Repair Locker 5, who in turn informed Damage Control Central. It's a very rapid pace. A ship's ability to remain afloat after sustaining damage is largely dependent upon a ship's feature called compartmentation. A ship's interior is divided into smaller spaces that can be secured and sealed. With this in mind, I immediately executed the carefully planned strategy and tactics I had been trained on. As I focused on the main problem, I also thought in the context of boundaries outside the affected space to keep damage contained by setting primary and secondary fire and smoke boundaries to prevent spread. I also considered all tools and resources at my disposal to formulate the best approach for each scenario.

My question is: how are you preparing and practicing for the most important roles you have in your life? Would it help to compartmentalize your situation, identify the root cause of an issue and implement sound strategies and tactics to overcome it? Complex situations become a lot easier to control when you discover the root cause and divide into separate manageable steps, but that takes careful thought and planning upfront.

discipline is the game-changer to win big

Everyone has a job to do, and everyone has to do it with the utmost excellence. Preparedness is the number one thing we look for from each shipmate. Everything and everyone counts since it's every single person's job to save the ship and preserve lives. Preparation is paramount for success, and it's a cinch to do behind the scenes when the pressure is off. Practicing makes us better prepared for handling complex issues in life. Always take the appropriate time to prepare. Things can and do get out of control quickly. The point I'm making is that everything counts, and practice makes it permanent.

fireproof strategies and tactics

Similar to a firestone, there will always be times when we need to withstand tremendous heat when the pressure is on. The strategies and tactics I learned as a Hull Technician-Damage Controlman in the U.S. Navy and as a volunteer firefighter/medic in New York are a transferable skill that I've employed in my personal and professional life, such as in developing cohesive sales teams, winning large strategic accounts and even working on school projects with my kids. Many people I know equate strategy and tactics with a military operation, since both terms were first used in the military. That makes sense. It seems lots of people use this technique with work projects, but I find few employ it to achieve their personal goals. It's a tremendously useful and simple tool to use to meet the demands of your personal life as well.

what is strategy? what are tactics? what's the difference?

On a basic level, Strategy focuses on the big picture — the Journey. An example might be planning a drive to New York City from North Carolina. If you get into a car and drive aimlessly, you'll likely never arrive. Who knows where you'll end up? Probably not in a good place, I would imagine. There's a lot more risk involved. Don't get me wrong; sometimes it's good to get lost, but not when you're on a focused journey.

Tactics focus on the small actions — the short distance steps. For example, using a GPS with a carefully planned number of road changes (tactics) at correct points, the outcome will be favorable. If you happen to veer off course for a short time, it's not a problem. Little risk involved. You make a correction and keep going, and you'll eventually arrive, guaranteed. It's good to cinch a guarantee, isn't it?

In the world of damage control aboard a ship, there is a multitude of things that can go very wrong, similar to a catastrophic event we may experience in our lives like losing a job or losing a loved one. If you've been burned before by a significant event, figuratively speaking, you'll know that some burns, although destructive at the time, can actually turn into a positive outcome. Just look at history. The Great Fire of London, for example, wiped out the city leaving behind only twenty percent of it, but also destroyed a deadly bubonic plague in the process.

Your ability to think clearly and act swiftly in this environment is critical for success and survival, and that comes with knowledge, preparation, massive action, and keeping things simple. The aim here is to achieve consistent personal growth, and that's done by developing an effortless strategic mindset.

a. strive to be an innate strategic thinker — come up with effective plans in line with your personal and professional objectives

b. before you begin with random tactics, take a moment and write down why you're doing them — think about the tactics' effectiveness

c. be sure your specific tactics are aligning with your strategies and you will always be a few steps ahead of everyone else.

This is a systematic process you can personally use on a routine basis. It helps to review personal and business issues, identify potential risks and opportunities, and perform long-term planning.

a. define strategy — WHY?
   • be as specific as possible

- remember, this is the driver for making decisions
b. identify metrics — HOW?
    - how do you know if you are on track or off track?
    - information is vital to measure results (baseline)
c. specify tactics — WHAT?
    - what is missing or needed that may be preventing you from realizing your journey
    - jettison ineffective, less productive tactics
d. ask for help — WHO?
    - find resources you can turn to.

IT'S A CINCH

CREATE BREAKTHROUGHS
AT WORK AND HOME

a. with the right priorities, the right things will happen
b. define your goals — be very specific
c. create an environment conducive for learning
d. let that inner child in you continue to live — don't allow adulthood to extinguish its flame
e. set boundaries and communicate — don't let things get out of control; compartmentalize issues and handle it
f. create itinerary — detailed calendar for work and home
g. all-hands-on-deck — delegate tasks; get the kids involved too
h. damage control central — a place for all information to post
i. create a binder containing vital documents for easy retrieval — how many times have you looked for that birth certificate?
j. find a place for everything — the seas do get rough
k. prevention — take immediate steps to eliminate hazards
l. take breaks to replenish and clear your mind — reward yourself.

Drinking water from a firehose can be overwhelming at higher velocities. Start slow and build up. Think like a firefighter, and at times, take a sip from a drip approach. When introducing something new, many people would rather play it safe and not try something new by itself. Introduce a new thing with something familiar. Blend it together. People are resistant to pressure. Do things when people are thirsty for new ideas. If they are thirsty, they'll be more willing to try new things.

NOTES
I am just one simple idea away

CINCH IT #2

LOST AND FOUND

"Why fit in when you were born to stand out?"
– Dr. Seuss

I n 1975-76, New York City was struggling financially and racked with high crime rates. It really became a wild concrete jungle in the late '70s and early '80s.

My family's financial struggles also showed real signs of trouble in the city. The business my dad worked for closed down a few years back, so he bartended and drove a yellow checkered taxicab. My mother was working for the city as a school crossing guard to make ends meet. Mayor Abraham Beame then laid off many thousands of city workers including police, fire, hospital workers, teachers and sanitation workers, and Mom lost her job with them.

It became known as "Stinky City" for a while, and chaos ensued.

One particular night the electricity in our apartment was turned off in Washington Heights because the bills couldn't get paid. Mom and Dad collected candles and flashlights to get us through for a couple of days until they could get the power back on. The food in the refrigerator also spoiled, since it stopped working. We were able to salvage the little we had because the apartment had a gas stove. After that scenario, I learned to choose gas over electricity for heating and cooking since you have an opportunity to keep going if the power ever goes out for whatever reason. Something to consider!

My brothers and I went to bed like normal that night, and both Mom and Dad headed out late. Mom said, "I need to go out for something, and I'll be right back," and we went to sleep.

KNOCK! KNOCK! KNOCK! A few hours later that night, we were abruptly woken by the banging on the apartment door. As we got out of bed, we walked quietly over to Mom and Dad's bedroom and noticed they weren't back yet.

KNOCK! KNOCK! KNOCK!

"Who is it," my older brother Billy asked.

"It's the Police. I need you to open your door," they said. "We are fine," Billy replied.

"I need you to open your door," the cop repeated.

Billy cautiously opened the door, keeping his body in position in case he needed to shut it quickly. The two cops at the door shined their flashlights on us and inside the apartment.

"Are your parents home?" they asked.

Billy went on to explain, "My father is at work and mother stepped out for a few minutes. She's on her way back."

"We were called to check on an odor of burning candles," they said, and asked a few more questions about Mom and Dad's whereabouts.

"Can you let us in? We just want to be sure everything's alright," they said.

They came in for a few moments to check on where the candles were located, and then told us to go with them until they could find our parents.

"Where are you taking us?" I asked.

"We'll take you boys down to a family center in lower Manhattan for a little while," the police officer said.

They were trying their best to make us feel comfortable. "If you like, we'll let you turn on the lights on the way down," one of them said. Pretend you are a cop tonight."

We all hopped in the back of the police cruiser. "Okay, hit the lights!" the driver said. He drove out of the neighborhood and headed down the exact same route Dad would take us to visit Grandma in Yorkville in his checkered taxicab; that was somewhat comforting. I have to admit, driving down the Harlem River and FDR Drive in the middle of the night in a police car was impressive. As nerve-racking as this was for us, it looked pretty cool seeing the police lights bouncing off the walls and reflecting on the East River water current. It definitely took our attention away from being in an upsetting situation. We didn't understand fully where we were being taken, but they made it sound like a good family center. It was far from that.

They placed us in the custody of New York City's Child Welfare System. My mother contacted the local police precinct when she found us missing, and she was notified that we had been taken from them and that they were being charged with endangering the welfare of a child and neglect, with possible prosecution. That was unfathomable for us. Despite our family being destitute and our parent's alcoholism issues, they couldn't love us more than they did. We were very close.

When we arrived at the center, a person at the facility gave us an exam. They separated my brothers and I and asked various questions to find potential signs of physical abuse or neglect. My brothers and I had no physical indicators of child abuse or neglect. Investigators were trying to discover what was going on and why. We tried many times to explain that there was nothing wrong — except for them taking us away. Nothing my family could say mattered to them.

What am I saying? Some things in life are not always as they seem. In the words of King Solomon, "To answer before listening — that is folly and shame." How often have we quickly judged a situation or person to learn we were completely wrong? We live in a superficial society with too much government intervention. The best advice I can give you as a parent is to protect your family from something like this happening. Become skilled at how to advocate for yourself and your family. Having someone come into your home and take your children away from you can be an overwhelmingly scary situation for anyone, especially if you had no idea something like this could happen.

My parents needed to go to Manhattan's Family Court and battle to get us back for what seemed like an eternity. To this day, I will never forget the fragrance of the soap they used in that foster care center, which I still recognize on occasion in some hotels or restaurant washrooms while traveling.

After a hard-fought battle with the city's family legal system, we were able to be released from foster care, and were temporarily placed in the custody of a church member's home. Thank God for the church we belonged to and the friends and associations we had there. The only caveat was this: my brothers and I needed to be temporarily separated during this time in order to make the release happen. Each of us were taken into a different church member's home in Yorkville Manhattan until the details can be sorted out with the court.

Other than feeling upset, violated and confused, for the most part, this decision turned out to be a blessing in disguise. Remember what I said about being burned, figuratively speaking, in a previous chapter? The bad has an equivalent seed of good. The wonderful people who took us in had beautiful homes and provided an opportunity to see another side of life. The grace and love these amazing people shared lit up a dark place. I was placed in the care of the rector at The Church of the Holy Trinity, and slept in the stunning rectory. The ambiance inside and outside is breathtaking. The rectory is a three-story parsonage attached to the church with an elegant main entrance. I felt so privileged and blessed to have the opportunity to be able to stay in such a beautiful, spiritual place. What made it extra special was being close to my fragile grandmother, who was always at the church doing volunteer work. She relocated from Bristol, England to Yorkville, NYC in the late 1920s and started attending the church immediately. In fact, Yorkville is where my mother and her siblings grew up.

I remember sitting on a sofa in the rectory watching television one day and impulsively turned to blurt out a question for my brothers, only to realize that nobody was in the room with me. Reality sunk in that I've been taken from my family. That's the first time I felt lost and alone, even though I was in one of the safest places on earth. It was a unique experience for me that I'll never forget. What I learned from that event was you cannot find your way in life until you are lost trying to figure things out. People can always help, but it's only you that can truly make that discovery.

There's a difference between being alone and being lonely. Being alone is a state of self-awareness; it's a positive encounter. On the other hand, loneliness is a state of being deficient; it's negative encounter. Through prayer and time spent in God's word, I've learned that we are never alone if we request God's assistance. Life takes you in unexpected directions — that's when you can actually learn the most about yourself and the Creator. In fact, just a couple of years ago during a visit to NYC, I was pleasantly surprised to see a large poster of my grandmother and I hanging in the chapel hallway referring to "community." I happened to be with friends and family during that visit, and we were all shocked to see the poster. Wow! That gave us chills.

An old German Proverb says, "Poverty is the sixth sense." One summer in 1980, my brothers and I were trying to figure out ways to make money in Yorkville so we could buy a few necessities like food and clothing, and also make it a bit easier on our parents since hard times kept spreading like the news. We were too young to be officially employed, and we wanted to find ways to serve people. Living in Manhattan all of our childhood, we had a knack for knowing what people appreciated since we had been exposed to very large diverse groups and situations. Maturity quickly caught up with us.

Spending time at dad's bartending job in the Hell's Kitchen area of Manhattan opened our eyes to quite a bit. We sat quietly in the back area observing everyone and everything. As we got a little older, we thought about that experience and recognized an opportunity to sell newspapers in bars. The patrons were usually joyful and spirited, sipping their cocktails and beers, and seemed to have money to spend. Plus, we had already figured out the "Why" we needed to make money, and this would be a great way to deliver a service in return. The remaining defining questions we asked ourselves were "Who, What, Where and How?"

Who: bars with affluent patrons — lower risk of finding trouble

What: Sunday's edition delivered Saturday night — fresh news

Where: Upper East Side (route was between the 70th Street and 90th Street, including 1st, 2nd and 3rd Avenues) — concentration of popular bars. In total, we canvassed around sixty city blocks, up three busy avenues each Saturday night.

The newspapers were a quarter apiece at the time, so we started with four papers each; all it took was $1 to get going. The next thing we needed to do was find out which newsstand in the neighborhood got the first deliveries that night, so we could get started earlier and have a greater chance to visit more places that were full of clients. It was a numbers game. Some Saturdays were busier than others. We dressed as best as we could and approached the bartenders and asked for their permission. They eventually got to know us, and they were accustomed to seeing us on Saturday nights. Since we didn't have much time to talk to potential buyers, we would quickly scan the paper's headlines and pictures searching for the most appealing ones to share that night, and we were in business.

We didn't have a selling price for the paper. We accepted whatever the customer thought was fair for what we shared. There was something for everyone: comics, headlines, sports, articles, puzzles, advertisements, etc. We were having a good run at this little enterprise and enjoyed meeting new people. This idea was shared with a couple of friends when they asked what we've been doing, and they immediately jumped on our idea. That's when you know you have a good one! The bars we were usually selling in eventually prevented any of us from selling inside because other kids weren't as respectful, and it became a nuisance for the patrons. Needless to say, we were disappointed. We then invested in bicycles and took our newspaper route further downtown, but it didn't provide as good results. I learned quickly that some people will take your idea and run away with it. It's a form of flattery, my older brother, Billy said. We thanked the bartenders for the opportunity and handed them thank you cards. "You Yorkville News Brothers were good," they said.

We always dared to try new ideas. The St. Patrick's Day Parade on 5th Avenue was incredible to attend. I loved going to all the parades in the city with my family; it's a memory I'll always cherish. The streets were packed with lots of people and festivities. The St. Patrick's Day Parade route would conclude in Yorkville on 86th street, and every business in the area was at full capacity. We thought this would be a great opportunity to sell green carnations for a day. We took the subway out to Woodside, Queens early in the morning because the carnations were a fraction of the price, and we purchased as many as we could afford. We added inexpensive ribbons and made them look awesome. They were a big hit! I wonder if the "Kiss Me I'm Irish" shirt we wore had anything to do with it?

This holiday idea led to another. Thanksgiving and Christmas time in New York City is a special time for everyone. Around mid-November, we would begin to see Christmas tree vendors sprout up on street corners. Billy approached one of the vendors on 86th Street in Yorkville and offered to deliver Christmas trees free of charge to their customers; we would simply work for tips. We were turned down by several vendors before finding a "yes." This particular vendor thought it would be a great service to compliment his business. "We'll provide excellent service, and we'll keep this area clean and inviting for customers," we promised, and did just that.

We would always make it a habit to go above and beyond their expectations. For example, we always positioned the Christmas tree so the best side was facing out in the home and got the thumbs up from the customer, added water in the basin, and reminded them never to let the tree dry out because they could easily catch fire. Many times I was offered hot chocolate, home-cooked meals, and money — it was a beautiful thing on a cold winter day. This local stand received many referred customers because of the valuable delivery service my brothers and I provided. They were outselling the other vendors that turned our free delivery service away by far.

The point I'm making here is to always be open to new ideas and learn different ways to serve others. Provide outstanding service regardless of your situation. What does the word OUTSTANDING mean to you? In Spanish, the word outstanding translates as exceptional or extraordinary. That's the reputation I want for myself in everything I do. Providing outstanding assistance both at home *and* work is the name of the game. That means always giving more than expected, and leaving a place better than the way you found it. These small opportunities allowed me to learn what people truly value and what it really means to serve others. Be well known for going the extra mile in everything you do. Everything.

IT'S A CINCH

HOW TO MAXIMIZE YOUR
INTERNAL COMPASS

a. what do you love to do?

b. where would you love to live?

c. what are you most thankful for?

d. what do you think about when you're by yourself?

e. if you lost everything tomorrow, who would you run to?

f. what can you try to do with no fear of failure?

g. where would you love to work?

h. who is already doing what you would love to do?

i. what are you naturally good or great at?

j. how can you serve others today?

Which answers align with your needs and which ones don't? In the end, after careful thought, research and counsel, it's only you who can decide what's right. Once you discover your true north, you and your loved ones will find that remarkable breakthroughs happen and doors will fly open. Sailors know magnetic north is not as accurate as true north. Magnetic north can get you close, but true north will take you *exactly* to your destination. Find your true north.

NOTES
I am just one simple idea away

CINCH IT #3

THE GOLDEN TICKET

"Stop thinking too much. It's alright not to know the answers. They will come to you when you least expect it."
– Unknown

The scene opens as Mrs. Bucket stands over a mountain of clothes, yet to be washed, as her son Charlie walks in.

Mrs. Bucket: Charlie, what are you doing here?

Charlie: I thought if you were ready, I'd walk you home.

Mrs. Bucket: I wish I were, but it looks like I'm going to be here late tonight.

Charlie: Oh. Well, I guess I'll be going then.

Mrs. Bucket: Well, why don't you stay a minute. Here, pull up a pile of clothes and sit down. Everything alright at school?

Charlie: Yep.

Mrs. Bucket: Good. Go on your newspaper route today?

Charlie: Just finished.

Mrs. Bucket: Good.

Charlie: I wanted to tell you something. They found the third ticket today.

Mrs. Bucket: Did they?

Charlie: Yea. Hmm. I guess I'll be going now.

Mrs. Bucket: Is that all?

Charlie: I just thought you would like to know. Most people are pretty interested. I know I'm interested. There are only two tickets left, you know. Just two. Pretty soon, just one.

Mrs. Bucket: I wonder who the lucky ones will be?

Charlie: In case you're wondering if it will be me, it won't be. Just in case you're wondering, you can count me out.

Mrs. Bucket: Charlie, there are 100 billion people in this world and only 5 of them will find golden tickets. Even if you had a sack full of money, you probably wouldn't find one. And after this contest is over, you will be no different from the billions of others that wouldn't find one.

Charlie: But I am different. I want it more than any of them.

Mrs. Bucket: Charlie, you'll get your chance. One day things will change.

Charlie: When? When will they change?

Mrs. Bucket: Probably when you least expect it.

from *Willy Wonka and the Chocolate Factory, 1971*
Roald Dahl

I recently watched one of my favorite family movies, *Willy Wonka and the Chocolate Factory*. The one with the late Gene Wilder as Mr. Wonka. The 1964 novel is a great read too, but this particular movie and soundtrack just takes your imagination to a higher place. Stories and movies are meant to move you. This story relates to my childhood — so much so, I resembled Charlie Bucket in appearance, disposition and circumstance.

As the beloved story goes, Charlie Bucket is a poor boy whose family is barely able to feed and support themselves. As good fortune has it, he found the last golden ticket and was selected as one of the five kids to tour the most popular and mysterious candy factory in the world. A suspicious stranger named Oscar Sluggworth attempts to get the winners to steal one Everlasting Gobstopper from the most secret candy making machine in the factory in exchange for wealth by putting Wonka and his factory out of business for good. Does Charlie take the bait, or does he become the "one" Wonka's been searching for to take over his factory?

What's interesting to know is that Peter Ostrum played Charlie Bucket in the original movie version when he was thirteen years old and never continued acting after that film, although he had multiple offers. He went on to study veterinary medicine and started a veterinary clinic. Both of my daughters love horses, so we saddled up and learned everything we could about them, and in the process, we rediscovered *Willy Wonka*. As we researched horses, we came across an article where Dr. Ostrum was interviewed in 2000 by the Journal of the American Veterinary Medical Association, and I'll never forget something he said in the interview regarding horses and how he got involved with veterinary medicine. Dr. Ostrum was introduced to horses by his father when he returned from Germany after filming *Willy Wonka*.

"I can remember the veterinarian coming out and taking care of the horses, and it made a huge impression on me," Dr. Ostrum said.

"This person really enjoyed what he did for a living. My father was a lawyer, and I really didn't have a clue what he did all day. But I knew *exactly* what the veterinarian did. Someone making a living from something he enjoyed so much really sparked my interest."[7]

This article resonated with me. Growing up, I would ask "what if" questions. What if my parents were lawyers? What if they were doctors? What if we had money? What would've become of us and our struggles? Here's a kid that had no real idea what his father did all day at work. I can imagine there are many more of you that don't know that answer. As a kid, I co-traveled with my dad in his taxicab and watched him bartend. The question I have for you is: what do your children know about your work? Why not take them along and show them? I've brought my kids with me to help while I worked health fairs. It was valuable exposure for them. They participated in the Juvenile Diabetes Walks and health fairs and bonded with wonderful people.

trust it will all work out – have no doubt

Never forget the golden ingredient — belief in yourself. Where the mind goes, energy flows. The best things in life happen when you least expect it. Sometimes love happens when you least expect it. An opportunity pops up when you least expect it. Friendships come into your life when you least expect it. A pregnancy comes when you least expect it.

You get a big customer when you least expect it. You may lose something that's been toxic when you least expect it. Never stop imagining. Close your eyes and open your mind to the possibilities.

Another unexpected "golden ticket" for me was the King Tut exhibit at the Metropolitan Museum of Art in 1978. We were later told that this exhibit was one of the hottest tickets in town. My brothers and I frequently spent time at museums to get off the streets and out of the cold — we practically lived in them year-round. We were very familiar with the layout. One December night The MET had all the glamour and spotlights out. There were lines of people as far as the eye could see, so we walked in the museum's service entrance and made our way to the famous exhibit hall. I was blown away by the historical artifacts, including the viewing of the gold funerary mask. It was majestic. One of the tour speakers was sharing information related to The Boy Pharaoh's life and treasure. What's fascinating to know is that he didn't accomplish much in his life, and yet, he was the most well-known pharaoh. Can you name another one off the top of your head? It's been said that he was given the throne around eight or nine years old. I was eleven years old standing in front of this mask in amazement, thinking, "what was his life like?" We all make assumptions. What crucial assumptions are you living under?

the art of self-education

As a kid, I had a huge interest in art and design. I began to pay closer attention to design and architecture; Central Park and the surrounding area was perfect for that. Exploring the museums and the city helped develop my self-education. When I learned to read better in school, I gained the confidence to apply to specialized high schools that were focused on teaching design. Like millions of other people in the U.S., I possessed weak reading skills and poor comprehension. That disadvantage was not likely to favor me, so I worked closely with educators. I needed help creating a place that was conducive to learning.

With the right focus in the right environment, I made major strides in a short period of time. It took lots of hours of practice and repetitive, purposeful reading, but I was able to raise my reading and comprehension by three grade levels in a single school year. One of the key lessons the educators shared was to be very clear about exactly what I was looking for in the reading. This same lesson applies to our lives; clarity and knowing exactly what we are after brings that particular thing or goal into focus. This simple concept opened a whole new world for me — literally! I've never looked at books and reading the same, and it's made a tremendous difference in my life and my career.

I also recruited the help of another teacher named Peter. We became friends, and I helped him and his wife paint their child's room in Brooklyn. He coached me in creating an art portfolio that I could compete with at The High School of Art & Design and The High School of Music and Art. He taught me how to cater to my talents to help me stand out from the crowd. We focused on personality, desires and ideas that inspired me, and of course, the school's requirements. Ultimately, I got accepted to A&D in NYC. I couldn't be more proud at the time. That achievement was a mighty wind in my sails.

My first year attending the competitive design school was a complete disaster for me. I failed all of my classes due to missing too many days of school because of the hardship at home. Eviction notices were never going to happen again in my life. The guidance counselor at A&D sat me in her room and laid the cards on the table.

She said, "Mr. Poole, there are many other students that want to attend A&D and are more than willing to take your seat. You have a serious choice to make if you want to graduate here. Tell me, do you want to stay at A&D?"

I said, "Yes, I need to be here."

"We'll need your full commitment — are you certain?" she said.

"Yes. I will do whatever I have to do," I said.

"You have one more chance to make it right," she said. I said, "Tell me how."

"You must retake your sophomore year by attending two night classes for the next two school years, and attend Saturday classes as well. You also must maintain your current workload at A&D," she explained.

"I will do it! Thank you for giving me a second chance," I said.

"I believe in you," she said as I left her office.

This temporary derailment turned out to be another blessing in my life. I met the toughest physical education teacher in one of my night classes, and he got me in top physical shape for the U.S. Navy. As a result of my make-up design classes on Saturday mornings, I attended programs at Cooper Union and Parson's School of Design and had the opportunity to learn new strategies and approaches in design that I wouldn't have learned otherwise. Allow me to share the "Olympic training" schedule from those days. I attended my normal grade schedule at A&D with a brand-new fervor, majoring in industrial design; attended Tuesday and Thursday evening classes; and attended Saturday classes for the next two calendar school years. I also started a life-changing part-time job at a local hospital supply pharmacy, and worked after school Monday, Wednesday, Friday, and a full day Sunday. I took naps on the subway and buses as I traveled back and forth. This tight schedule also kept me from getting into too much trouble in the gutter.

The four most powerful questions the school taught me to ask myself when making key decisions were:

a. why do I want to be a part of?
b. what are my expectations?
c. who really inspires me and why?
d. what motivates me to give my best every day and work hard?

Having well thought out answers to these simple questions was critical for me since I had many obstacles to over- come, and the answers I wrote down helped me to remain in the game and never quit. When life gets tough, as it will at some point for all of us, we need to hold tightly on to something that will keep us going forward, because it's very easy to give up.

IT'S A CINCH

SEEK A MENTOR FOR WORK AND HOME

a. the Golden Ticket is Self-belief
b. understand yourself — how do you work best?
c. identify someone you admire and respect
d. learn where to look for a mentor
e. decide what you need in a mentor — be specific
f. ask them about their greatest challenges
g. agree on mutual expectations
h. create to a monthly meeting goal to measure success
i. have an attitude of gratitude — show appreciation
j. take advantage of all of your resources
k. remember that people are willing to share their expertise
l. focus on the family
m. look for opportunities to build your relationships
n. never quit — success is closer than we think.

I've made mistakes, even big ones, but have learned that we always have another chance to do it right the next time. It's amazing how things always work out when you have a good disposition and the right people within your inner circle. Combine this with the Golden Ticket, Self-belief, and you will find your way out of any tough situation. Remember: inch-by-inch, anything's a cinch.

NOTES

I am just one simple idea away

SECTION TWO:
SUPPORT AND MIRACLES

CINCH IT #4

LET ME SEE YOUR I.D.

*"Never forget what you are, for surely the world will not.
Make it your strength. Then it can never be your weakness.
Armour yourself in it, and it will never be used to hurt you."*
– George R.R. Martin, Game of Thrones

D ad had a wonderful sense of humor. He also had a way with words. Mom called it "the gift of gab." I remember him saying to me, "Bobby, if you don't know what you're doing, ask someone!" and "Up and at 'em," including "There ain't nobody here but us chickens," as he smiled. In fact, I found him saying the same things to my daughters. When it came to choosing to bartend or drive a taxicab on a given night, he'd always choose to bartend. He would tell us the taxicab was expensive to operate, difficult to earn money with, and dangerous. He's seen his fair share of danger in WWII and Korean War. He was a farm boy from Clayton, NC. One night shift, while working his taxicab, he picked up a passenger who had violent motives. The passenger attempted to rob and kill him by slitting his throat with a knife as he was driving away. Miraculously, he was able to leap out of his taxicab while pushing the gas pedal, and it crashed with the thug inside. Dad was small in stature, but tough as nails.

Over time, the wounds healed and he began looking for work through a temporary employment agency in Manhattan. The temp agency eventually found him a delivery position at a busy pharmacy-hospital supply business called Clayton & Edward across the street from New York Hospital on Manhattan's Upper East. The temp agency seemed to have a difficult time placing reliable people there. My dad worked at the pharmacy business for a few weeks and became well-liked by clients. He was very trustworthy, so the pharmacy owners offered him a permanent delivery position. Soon after turning fifteen years old, I was also hired part-time; that's how I began getting involved with the medical industry.

The Upper East Side is a mecca for medical research where world-renowned researchers and medical professionals work and reside. In between stocking shelves, I also delivered specialty medicine and medical supplies to area hospitals and their respective pharmacies and patient care units, nursing homes and home health patients. The experience made an indelible impression on me. What made this work-life relationship very favorable, particularly with the intense schedule at school was the store's location, the operating hours and an opportunity to work beside my dad. What a perfect scenario for me!

get out of jail free card

One Friday evening in June 1985, I was working at the store.

"Bobby, I have a delivery to make on the way home, I'll see you there," Dad said as we closed the store.

"Alright, I'll get classwork done before I head home," I replied.

I went to eat at the local pizza shop to get a project done for my Saturday After School Occupational Skills Program at Parsons School of Design. The pizzeria had a larger table for me to work on and they didn't mind me hanging out. They were customers, too. At home, I would use an empty dresser drawer as a drafting table; it was a piece of treasure I found on the street near work. I was able to tuck it under the pullout couch my brothers and I slept on to save space in the small apartment. This particular homework assignment was for one of the design classes I needed to retake. Between work and school, some nights felt longer than others — I was out of the house fourteen hours every weekday and eleven hours on the weekends. Thank God for Thanksgiving and Christmas holidays!

After about four hours of doing homework at the pizzeria, I boarded the Second Avenue city bus to go home, which took much longer than normal because of traffic near the 59th Street Bridge that connected Manhattan and Queens. I usually fell asleep on the bus and would somehow awake just in time to hop off on Allen and Rivington Street in the Lower East Side. On occasion, I'd accidentally wake up too late and walk back, passing CBGB's hardcore punk rock crowd. This particular nap put me in a stupor that night. As I turned onto Ludlow Street, I noticed a group of humongous rats feeding on a large trash bag outside a bodega. Alley cats don't even mess with these rats. Incidentally, this was the same street corner the hip-hop group Beastie Boys used on their classic Paul's Boutique Album from 1989. Of course, there was no real Paul's Boutique there; they changed it for the cover. I remember leaping on to the street so I can avoid the infected city dwellers feasting on the garbage.

A short "WHOOP-WHOOP" sound came from a nearby car.

An unmarked police car noticed me in the middle of the street under the street lamp light and stopped me.

"Police! Stop there!" the undercover cops yelled.

Both men approached me with each of their hands at their holster side and asked: "What are you doing on the street?"

"I'm trying to get to my building," I said while looking behind me where the rats were eating aggressively.

"Hey, face me! Where do you live?" the cop said. "123 Ludlow Street," I said.

"Show me your I.D.?" the cop said.

As I was looking through my pockets and portfolio case, I realized I didn't have any form of I.D. apart from my library card.

"Here you are, Sir," I said while handing the card over. "How old are you?" they asked.

"I'm seventeen, Sir," I replied.

One cop turned to the other and said, "This is a library card!"

"Where are you coming from?" they asked. "From school and work," I said.

"Where's that?" they asked.

"70th Street and York Avenue," I said.

That's when it dawned on me — they thought I was up to no good since this area was known for heroin dealing. In the 1980s, the Lower East Side, or "Loisaida" in Spanish, was largely Hispanic and no other white kids lived on that street — at least that I was aware of. My brothers and I were a few of the only non-Hispanic kids attending the Junior High School down the street, if I recall correctly.

"Show us your apartment," they said.

"But, it's almost midnight, and my parents are asleep," I responded.

"Show us!" they said.

It was an old tenement building with tiny apartments. They were so small; the bathtub was located in the kitchen opposite of the stove and small refrigerator and included a makeshift toilet enclosure in the same space. We lived on the third floor, and you could clearly hear the police radio chatter in the quiet stairway. Surprisingly, my mom was awake waiting for me to get home from work since Dad had been there for hours. I heard her coughing in the kitchen where the front door was located. Mom opened the door to see me standing outside with two cops behind me.

"Is something the matter?" She said with a puzzled look. "Everything is fine, Mom," I said.

"Sorry for the intrusion, ma'am. We needed to verify your son's residence." the cop explained.

"Did he do something wrong?" Mom asked.

"No, ma'am. We noticed him on the street, and we were suspicious. This area isn't the safest place at night," the cop said.

"Here's your I.D.," the cop said while handing me my library card.

get out of jail free card

Although it may not have looked exactly like this situation, I think it's safe to say all of us have been scrutinized about who we are at some point in our life; whether in a job interview, a college interview, when joining the military, etc. Each of us has created a personal identity to some degree, especially with the advent of social media. The social media notes and pictures we put out add to that identity. Appearance matters. How do you define yourself? What identity are you striving to hold on to? What are your qualities and beliefs that distinguish you?

both potential and transferable skills *are* powerful

While in college, I continued to work at the specialty pharmacy as well as New York Hospital's engineering department as a preventive maintenance mechanic, but had a strong desire to get experience in an advertising and graphic design company. A college friend introduced me to a start- up company called Image Axis, in the hustling Flatiron district in Manhattan. It was another unexpected opportunity. I interviewed with both partners of the business. Both were sharp-dressed men and highly articulate. We made some small talk before getting into the interview process, as one of them quickly asked a direct question: "Looking at your resume, I see you have ZERO experience in this business. Why should we hire you?"

What process do you think I followed to answer that? You got it: the four points I previously mentioned in CINCH IT #3: The Golden Ticket. It went something like this.

a. "I've met several of your customers, and they've all said great things about your creative work. In addition, I want to be a part of a leading team that's blazing the trails in advertising and graphic design, such as yours. My expectations are to learn quickly and begin producing results early."

b. "The person that motivates me to get up every day and do my best is my grandmother, Bessie. She emigrated here from Bristol, England with nothing to declare but her desire and will to improve her life. That really inspires me."

c. "Lastly, you make a valid point; I am limited on experience in this business. However, everyone has to begin somewhere. What I do have is an abundance of potential and a tremendous work ethic. I will not be outworked by anyone."

They both looked at each other while reclining back in their chairs and said, "We need a Navy guy like you here to kick some ass — when can you start?" Their top sales representative nicknamed me "Military," and it stuck. They never called me by my formal name again. My library card paid "dividends" once again when I used it to research the landscape in that industry at the New York Public Library.

squeeze the juice from your library card

I recently provided coaching to a friend to help with an important job interview she was preparing for.

"Let me ask you a question. Do you have a library card?" I said.

She replied, "No, I actually don't. Haven't been to the library in ages."

That's a common answer I get from people when I ask that question, and I find it fascinating. I may go on to quote Albert Einstein, since he's recognized by all: "The only thing that you absolutely have to know, is the location of the library." I'll then get responses such as, "What's the point, I'll Google what I need," or "It's out of the way" and "I don't have time."

How about the internet? Does the local public library offer off-site access? It's likely they do. I like to think about how Albert Einstein would have used the internet if he were alive today. Would he have? Just a thought. My wife, Maria is a huge Jane Austen, *Pride and Prejudice* fan, so in the spirit of Mr. Darcy, "I cannot comprehend the neglect of a family library in days as these."

On that note, don't neglect to connect with the world's largest library, The Library of Congress. If you have a question or need assistance, TLC offers an online "Ask a Librarian" service. Here's the thing. Librarians are trained to research and locate that specific book, DVD, CD or download you are seeking, so be sure to ask away. That information could possibly help you to land that great job, or save your business, marriage, or your health and wealth. A librarian can help you avoid the stress of information overload. Love the librarian! They are an underutilized resource.

Here's a glimpse of what you are missing if you are not taking advantage of your library card and the library's **FREE** online portal:

a. **business databases:** find new customers, analyze a market, evaluate competition, target media and direct mail campaigns

b. **company research:** compete and get that job or promotion, network, identify leadership and financial history, business to business leads, marketing and business planning

c. **investing:** possible real-time investment research, stock information, search for overall business climate within a given industry

d. **job & career:** veterans, career services, resumes, career workshops and local job listings

e. **children and parents:** resources for preschool and school-age children, librarian resource recommendations, search for ideas for science experiments and art

f. **local assistance:** many libraries include other agencies and organizations throughout the local community to provide in-depth services and support, expert advice, mentoring, networking opportunities and financial assistance

g. **marketing & demographics:** determine and research your target market; study an industry, scan for niche opportunities and create professional-quality maps and reports

h. **starting a business:** information for entrepreneurs and researchers, business cases, start-up planning

i. **continuing education and life-long learning:** online self-paced continuing education courses; videos, lectures, interactive programs; technology, literacy; math skills, etc.

j. **download** audiobooks, e-Books and free music

k. **language learning:** large variety of language courses

l. **genealogy:** search your family history

m. **nature and environment:** workshops & programs

n. **book clubs:** variety of networking opportunities with readers

o. **teens:** teen health, college prep, career guides, home-work help, comics and anime — create your own comic and gaming

p. **homework help:** current events, literature, magazines & newspapers, history science and test preparation

q. **government:** US Government, local and state governments, resources in other states, census and voter information

r. **nonprofit:** fund-raising, search for grants, grant-writing, and start-up and management of nonprofit organizations

s. **volunteer opportunities:** great place to give back.

"There is no problem a library card can't solve."
– Eleanor Brown

IT'S A CINCH

HOW TO CREATE BREAKTHROUGHS AT WORK AND HOME

a. protect your personal identity — build your personal brand

b. take responsibility of your attitude and actions — feel good

c. always treat people with respect regardless of status — you never know who you'll meet on the way up or down

d. maintain a good appearance — good thoughts over bad ones

e. refine your character traits and be the best you can be

f. minimize external influences that can harm your creative mindset and wellbeing

g. demonstrate your expertise — find a way to show it, don't tell

h. connect with people and groups and share ideas

i. make a good first impression

j. get involved in extra projects and learn

k. break the habit of getting stuck — it's never too late to change something

l. be determined and find what compliments your skills and values

m. identify problems and offer ideas to solve them.

Discovering opportunities that identify with your interests and beliefs can be stressful, but it's remarkably rewarding when you do. How do we do that, exactly? We always find ways to do something if we are convinced enough; if not, we'll find excuses. What are you reading? Are you reading enough? Mark Twain said, "The person who doesn't read is no better off than the person who can't read." You may be familiar with the phrase "birds of a feather flock together." Network with people and volunteer in the area you are highly interested in when possible. Visit your local chamber of commerce and meet people. Read your local business papers (FREE) at the library and find out who the movers and shakers are in your respective field. Ask them to mentor you. You are naturally tuned-in to all the opportunities of life, so remain hopeful. The impossible can and does happen. Believe that you can beat all the odds against you — many have proven that time and time again, including myself.

NOTES
I am just one simple idea away

CINCH IT #5

INTUITION

"The gift of Intuition keeps on giving, if only we listen."
– Robert Louis Poole, CINCHOLOGY®

On Monday, December 21, 1987, I was working aboard the ship for a pre-deployment exercise in the Mediterranean. I was off duty early and decided to walk around the Waterside Area of Downtown Norfolk VA, when I had a sudden sense that I needed to call my mom. The only way for me to reach her was at work, since there wasn't a telephone in the apartment. At the time, she was working for the New York City Department of Health in Brooklyn as an office aid. Some things in life are simply not explainable, such as instincts and intuition. That particular day, my inner voice spoke to me loud and clear.

"Hello, this is Robert Poole, calling for Helen Poole," I said to the woman who answered.

She responded, "Are you the son in the Navy?" "Yes, ma'am," I said.

She said, "One moment, please."

A different voice picked up the line: "I'm sorry to tell you this, but something terrible happened to your mother, and she was just taken by ambulance to the hospital. Just moments ago."

"Where did they take her?" I asked.

The new woman responded, "She had trouble breathing and fainted. I think they are taking her to Long Island College Hospital."

"Thank you for letting me know," I said. "We are all very sorry," she said.

I got on the payphone again to call the pharmacy to let my dad know what I had just learned. He was out on a delivery, so I left a message. I returned to my ship to let my leadership team know what was going on. Later that afternoon, I was able to get some information that my mom was admitted to the critical care unit. She just turned 53 years old, twelve days prior. I immediately visited the local American Red Cross to take out an interest-free hardship loan so I could get to New York and help my family. The American Red Cross also facilitated communication with my command and the hospital, so I could focus on my family. Many military members rely on the Red Cross for assistance — it's a phenomenal organization.

I arrived at the hospital, and my family was at the bedside. Mom was placed on life support. The ventilator was delivering breaths for her since she was unable to do it on her own. The doctor came into the room while we were there and shared information with us.

"It appears she had a cardiac arrest and severe oxygen deprivation. Intervention was delayed. Her blood didn't circulate well, and neither did her oxygen delivery," he said. I was told that CPR wasn't performed until the medics arrived. It took some time for help to arrive. Every minute a person waits for CPR after a cardiac arrest, the chances of survival are reduced dramatically.

"What are the chances of recovery?" I asked.

The doctor paused and said, "We'll have to wait and see."

I stayed at the hospital every day for the next two weeks, praying for a miracle. She showed no signs of life the entire time. It was one of the most difficult moments of our lives. The medical staff at the hospital began to discuss possible ethical decisions of ending the life support efforts. My dad and I were both faced with very difficult decisions. He was asked to consider pulling Mom's life support, and I was scheduled for a six-month deployment to the Mediterranean and needed to return to my ship in Little Creek, VA.

The morning I was to return to my ship, I stood beside Mom and debated to myself whether I should stay at her bedside or return to my ship. I had no liberty or time left and would face serious missing ship movement charges if I didn't report for duty. As I leaned over, holding her hands, I faithfully prayed out loud for strength, guidance and an answer as I was contemplating my decision. I was preparing my mind to take on anything and everything. Sometimes we realize that our own strength is not enough to get us through a difficult situation, and we need something higher to hold onto for help. As I was praying to God almighty, I noticed an ever so slight movement of her head. Her pillow gave way enough for her head to move toward me as if she was trying to say something, but her eyes were completely shut. At that moment, while I was still holding her hands, I felt a sense of love, peace and power flow through my body. I stood there in silence with her and took it all in. That instant, I knew exactly what I needed to do.

I whispered to her, "You are in a better place now, and everything here will be fine. I will never quit making a better life for our family, and I will always cherish the moments we had."

I kissed her forehead and said, "I love you with all my heart and thank you for the gift of life. I will always make the best of it."

After adjusting her pillow, I left to report back to my ship.

you are stronger than you know

It had been two weeks since returning to the ship, and I thought about my family every moment of every day. I was preoccupied with workflow, and it helped. A lot of planning and preparation goes into deployments — in the event that we need to fight. On Saturday, January 16th, my ship was contacted by the American Red Cross that my mom passed on her own will. I had a very small window of time to fly home and help with the funeral arrangements. As the word quickly spread aboard, unbeknownst to me, my shipmates passed a hat around the command to collect money for me to take care of my family. There's a strong bond in the military community; you become a very tight-knit group.

We all have an inner voice that speaks to us in the form of intuition and gut instincts. What is yours trying to tell you? Learn to listen to it. When my intuition or instincts tell me something, I've learned to pay close attention and balance what it's telling me and how I should act on it. It's a powerful force, and if you ignore it, you may pay a high price. It can also help you avoid a really bad situation. For example, there was a day I went to work and something unexplainable inside told me, "Take the bus today to work instead of the subway." When I got to work, the radio was playing in the back room of the pharmacy and a news flash came on about a building collapse on Delancey Street on the Lower East Side. It turned out to be the same route I normally take to work. The front end of the building collapsed into the street about the same time I was to walk past it.

a. learn to understand the messages and signals your mind and body are communicating — create down time and solitude
b. balance is important — trust your gut and balance it with your experience and knowledge and make the best choice

    c. view and sense everything — situational awareness is a tremendous skillset I learned in the U.S. Navy; put the smart phones away and "sense" everything that's going on around you.

learn CPR and First Aid

After Maria and I were married, we decided to support families in need as it related to teaching first aid and CPR programs in the memory of my mother, so we started a company called BOO-BOO, LLC. We both were certified as Emergency Medical Technicians with a special emphasis on cardiac defibrillating equipment. I also became a certified instructor for the American Red Cross, and a recognized training agency for the National Safety Council's First Aid Institute. We served families that couldn't afford professional training and provided it free of charge. We supplemented the expenses by selling custom first aid kits and training in the private sector and contracted with a company to market a cardiac event monitoring service to cardiology physician practices.

We did all of this around our college studies and full-time jobs prior to our first daughter being born. We met so many wonderful families and professional first responders in the process and were getting the attention of local media by writing and sharing articles on the lurking dangers in a home and first aid tips. That created more exposure with a television network. I was approached by a television producer asking if they could follow us around one of our home trainings, but schedules seemed to always conflict. I've learned a great deal from this process. The biggest problem we faced with this particular venture was that it required a major amount of one-on-one consulting, with little return on investment. We were trading hours for dollars with no residual income. With a new baby on the way and expenses piling up, we needed to refocus our attention and make some tough choices.

IT'S A CINCH

DEALING WITH HARD CHOICES
AT WORK AND HOME

a. create a plus and minus evaluation sheet — divide sheet in two rows

b. control feelings and keep negative emotions in check

c. who will this decision affect and how?

d. is it right for myself? Is it right for my family?

e. do I need a support system to talk it through? If so, who?

f. what's the worst that can happen in this scenario?

g. what does my gut tell me?

h. what can I do to distract myself to find an answer?

i. how can I stay connected with people?

j. what are my top constraints or priorities?

k. can I deal with the fall-out?

l. sleep on it and pray about it when possible.

Making difficult choices will always be present since life is so unique and dynamic. Make it a CINCH and write down what needs to be accomplished on the top of a blank page and set a deadline for yourself on the bottom of the page. In the center, create a road map. Make use of symbols and abbreviations for efficient note taking such as minus signs, equal signs, up arrows, down arrows, question marks, asterisk, v. for very, vv. for extremely, vs. for against, imp for important, eval for evaluation, etc.; anything to get the creative juices flowing. Making difficult choices needs a favorable and creative mindset. Lastly, select from your options, decide on the best approach, and take action.

NOTES
I am just one simple idea away

CINCH IT #6

UNBOUNDED PLEASURE

"Every dog must have his day."
– Jonathan Swift

I've learned so much from my dogs over the years. They are natural teachers demonstrating unrestrained enjoyment and love. One of these dogs that changed my life was Max. He helped me reconnect with life's little treasures — like fun-filled summer days playing in the city, true companionship and unconditional love. In fact, Max made it possible for me to meet the love of my life.

One of my cousins called me out of the blue needing a place to stay for a few days. The first night he stayed, I found him sound asleep on the floor in the foyer with a pile of poop near his head when I returned from work and class.

There was a puppy laying in the corner that came up to me as I walked into the apartment.

"Hey, little buddy," I said as I lifted him.

"What's with the puppy? I asked as my cousin woke up. "Someone was giving puppies away at the pub down the street, and I took one," he said.

They both stayed with me for a few more days. I quickly got attached to the puppy since he never left my side, and I named him Max. He was a beautiful lab mix with orange and white markings. The veterinarian told me to never leave him alone; someone may steal him. His beautiful white chest had the shape of a tuxedo shirt, and he even had two white paws that resembled a pair of white boots, so we called him Maxi Boots. Max and I would go to the local park in Woodside Queens so we could burn off some energy, and I met an older woman named Linda that had a young German Shepherd called She-Ra. We all became good friends, and the two dogs spent a lot of time together. Max loved She-Ra. After getting to know each other, Linda said, "You know, I think I have the perfect girl for you."

"Thank you, Linda. But, between full-time work and full-time college, I don't have any time left in a day for a relationship," I said.

After a few months of observing Max and She-Ra enjoy each other so much, I said, "Linda, would you mind introducing me to that girl you mentioned?"

"No problem, I'll give her a call. She's a family friend," she replied.

I'll admit, I didn't get off to a very good start. I received Maria's phone number and called her when I got home from work and class, but it was around 10:30 at night.

"Robert, do you realize the time? My parents are wondering why the phone is ringing this late and my baby sister is sleeping," she said.

Regrettably, I didn't consider the time when I called, since it was the only time where I was free and had access to a phone. I apologized profusely. Sometimes we neglect to use common courtesy like giving your full attention to the person you are interacting with; or saying please and thank you. Fortunately, Maria was fine with the late call, but it didn't make a good first impression. It helped that Linda thought fondly of me, so I was able to get past the phone screen and onto a date.

I remember watching Maria for the first time when she walked down the street. She looked amazing with her pretty smile, beautiful hair, and pink colored blouse. After meeting her, I felt that this was a dream come true. I eventually had an opportunity to introduce Max to her, and he was equally happy. A dog's instincts are usually right. As it turned out, She-Ra was Maria's dog originally. She-Ra was given to Linda before she relocated to Woodside Queens. The puppy love connection made our family possible! Good things really do come to us when we least expect it.

some chances may be slim, but anything is possible

Maria and I were planning on starting a family, and we both decided that no matter what, one us would put our career on hold to raise the children. One weekend, we were getting the baby room ready as she was getting close to giving birth to our first daughter. I was using my artistic talents to turn the baby room into a wondrous Winnie the Pooh and Tigger forest by painting a mural. My mom

loved Piglet, so I had to include him in her memory. As we were listening to a local classic rock radio station, they were having a fundraising event to help families on Long Island. They were auctioning off some incredible instruments and other cool pieces of memorabilia. One of the pieces auctioned was an electric guitar signed by Pete Townshend and Roger Daltrey from a legendary band, *The Who*.

"Maria, I am going to call into the radio station and win that guitar," I said convincingly.

"Small chance, but you have luck!" she said.

About an hour later, the radio DJ returned from a set list, and they were talking about *The Who* describing the signed guitar. No more than a couple of minutes later, I heard my name come over the radio: "Robert Poole from Massapequa Park, you are the winner of this electric guitar! Thank you for your contribution. Visit the event location to claim your prize!"

Maria and I looked at each other, and she said, "WOW!"

With a smile and a hug, I then replied, "Don't ever doubt me."

labor of love experiences

The climb to a new career in medical device sales was slow and laborious. During this time, I was still working towards my bachelor's degree at night, although I was nearly complete. There were many great interviews, but a majority of these corporations required a minimum of a bachelor's degree, and all the other candidates I competed with had one (or more). My specialized military experience had no bearing with their human resources — we still need to find a way to change that policy. Military experience is powerful for any career. Four years of specialized active duty service should equate to four years of college education. However, no matter how slim the chances were, I never gave up and was eventually hired as a sales representative specializing in respiratory acute and anesthesia care in hospitals. It was about the time that Maria was due to give birth. We both experienced labor pain together so to speak; of course, her labor was much grander.

"Robert, I think my water broke, please call the doctor," Maria called out calmly as she went to the bathroom.

I paged the physician, and she got on the telephone with him. "Hi, Doctor... Oh... It definitely came down now," she said.

He said, "I'll see you both at the hospital."

We grabbed our prepacked bag and headed out the door. She was feeling very comfortable, and there was a Dunkin Donuts on the way, so I said, "there's no traffic this late, let's stop quickly on the way to get some donuts for the nurses." She gave me a funny look. "The nurses are our new best friends," I said.

As the woman in the donut shop came to the window to collect the money, she asked, "How are you folks tonight?"

I replied gleefully, "We are doing better than good, my wife's water broke, and we're having a baby soon!"

The lady's eyes got wide as she tossed the donut boxes into the car and said: "It's okay, you can go."

"But I need to pay you," I replied.

Her eyes somehow got even wider and her voice deeper: "No! Get your wife to the hospital, go, go!" as she swooshed her hand.

I looked over to my wife, and she yelled, "let's go!"

Off we went.

We quickly arrived at the birthing center and handed over the donuts at the nurse's station as they got us all set up in a birthing room. The nurses all had smiles that lit up the room.

Maria's physician came into the room and said, "thanks for the donuts — nice touch," with a smile and a wink.

I immediately put on hospital scrubs, washed up and stayed by Maria's side. As we sat there waiting, we reflected on the journey that brought us to this moment. During the entire pregnancy, I only missed one appointment with her, and that's exactly how I dreamed it would be. Early in the pregnancy, she was having complications and we were referred to a high-risk perinatologist, which required many additional visits. Maria resigned from her job at the hospital and put her nursing education on hold to avoid any complications.

Our game plan was to always have a stay-at-home parent, but a little later in the process. The sudden changes caused us some financial burdens initially since I took a big financial hit with the entry-level medical sales job. Some of our family members and close friends thought I was making a bad choice leaving a higher paying job for an unknown risky career during this time, and many tried talking me out of it. I know they all loved us and meant well. Although I had enormous faith and courage that we would make it, having a supportive spouse puts an extra spring in your step. I felt unstoppable with her by my side, and still do.

"Can't believe it's been almost fifteen hours since your water broke," I said.

"I want to have this baby," Maria said.

"We are almost there! You are amazing," I responded. The doctor positioned himself at the foot of the bed, called me over, and told me to get ready. The nurse took my previous place to help Maria push.

Soon after, I began to see the baby's head crown for the first time, and I was in awe. What a miracle!

"Our girl is coming out, my love!" I said as tears of joy streamed down my face.

The baby's head was now out, and the doctor suctioned the mucus from the nose and mouth, then her other arm, and the rest of the body followed.

The baby's umbilical cord was clamped, and the doctor said, "Robert, cut the cord!"

This was truly the most remarkable thing that's ever happened to me in my life. Seeing your baby born first-hand is truly a gift from God.

The physician says with glee, "Here's your beautiful daughter. Congratulations." Regrettably, they couldn't place the baby on Maria's chest for 24 hours since both mom and baby spiked a severe fever. That was also tough. Immediately after Maria gave birth, the baby was whisked to isolation for 24 hours to monitor. Maria's maternal instincts quickly triggered and she told me to leave her and stay with the baby. Amazing woman!

The saying "Labor brings new life" has a whole new meaning for me. Big goals in life truly require a concerted effort. The question I have for you is: What does your dream team look like to bring your dreams to life? The know-how and skills shared by the clinical team during the entire pregnancy were powerful. We've nurtured incredible skills, such as improved breathing techniques to remain calm; keeping focused by always having our eye on the prize (the baby); and the desire to give it all we've got to make it all come together.

Then, suddenly a day comes after you've thought it was too much to handle and would never do it again, and boom, the miracle process starts again.

Sixteen months later another miracle occurred in our life. Maria and I had the opportunity to experience this amazing process one more time when she got pregnant with our second daughter. The doctors were very cautious because of her first go around and sadly experiencing the heartache of a miscarriage in between. I was astonished to learn that one in every five pregnancies ends in a miscarriage. The most difficult part of the prenatal experience for us was the world of the unknown — would she carry the whole term? We can't always predict the twists and turns in life, but we can certainly learn how to best plan and handle them.

As time passes and we get busy with our lives, it's easy to forget the beauty around us. Take time to cherish family. Let people know that you appreciate them. When things get busy, put your family before friends. Do fun things together. Communicate openly. Eat together every chance you get. Plan a date with your spouse or partner or take your kids out for ice cream. Take time to get to know your kids' friends — know who they're hanging out with.

Create memorable times. For example, when we relocated to North Carolina from New York for a job opportunity, we wanted to meet new people sooner than later since we didn't know anyone. We were starting from scratch, so we planned a couple of simple pizza parties with a "Magic at the Movies" theme for our daughter's new schoolmates. We even rolled out a red carpet at the front door and invited parents, siblings of classmates, the school bus driver and the teachers. Most everyone invited came.

It was amazing. We all made wonderful friendships and memories, and even exchanged business cards to help one another succeed at home and work.

IT'S A CINCH

HOW TO PREPARE FOR A BABY
AT WORK AND HOME

A growing family can be very stressful. One way to reduce stress is to plan as early as possible. Communication is important to manage through all the important issues that will arise. Initially, small changes may be necessary to adjust for the pregnancy. For my family, we needed to make big changes early on because of the work demands placed on us and the complex pregnancies we experienced.

a. create a journal and establish priorities
b. figure out what you need
c. reign in frivolous spending and create a budget
d. get familiar with your benefits plan at work
e. ask your physician's office and hospital for medical estimates — we experienced surprise medical charges not covered by our health insurance plan and it was costly
f. create an exit strategy or plan for maternity leave — communicate with management and clients

g. get a term life insurance policy in place
h. write a will
i. take time for each other
j. evaluate childcare options
k. ask for help
l. use your local library and toy library to save money
m. bring baby blankets home from hospital to let pets smell.

A lot happens in a short period of time. Every month is a new experience and a new challenge. It's important to be supportive and helpful in all areas to reduce stress and worries, especially for mama bear. And dads to be, don't ever feel left out. Enjoy the miracle process — nothing compares to it. Lastly, remember to read and bond with the bump. It is priceless.

NOTES
I am just one simple idea away

SECTION THREE:
GROWTH AND FOCUS

CINCH IT #7

SHORTCUTS AND IVY LEAGUE

"There are shortcuts to happiness and dancing is one of them."
– Vicki Baum

I n between dancing at annual national sales meetings and enjoying the destination, I am often asked about shortcuts to success and happiness; do they really exist? Some people say there are no shortcuts to real success. If there are shortcuts to real failure like cheating and cutting corners to get a job done, shouldn't there be an equal opposite of doing something efficient? I tend to believe good shortcuts to success do exist. I'm not referring to being in a hurry with a get rich quick thing. That doesn't exist unless you hit a mega lottery, and research shows that usually has disastrous results. There are effective shortcuts we can take advantage of in nearly every aspect of our life.

History has revealed success stories where people have already paved the way and made mistakes that we can benefit from. Some say it's good to discover mistakes on your own, because of the lessons you can gain from them. That's a true statement. I've learned a tremendous amount on my own by making mistakes over the years, even big ones, and also learned there are better and easier ways to do things. Going a shorter route shouldn't always mean you are taking the proverbial low road. Since there seems to be a stigma associated with taking shortcuts, I would like to challenge you to look at them as an "alternative route" or a "time-saving method."

For example, learning from other people's successes and failures saves a lot of time, and I am in the school of thought to use that to my advantage. In fact, research shows this to be the truth. Have you ever had a friend tell you when you were shopping, "I wouldn't buy that 'widget' if I were you. It broke down so many times and cost so much, I could've bought three of the other model." Our brains respond to that feedback more favorably than if we went through the process and made the mistakes on our own. There was interesting research done at the University of Bristol called *I Win, You Lose: brain imaging reveals how we learn from our competitors.*[8] It revealed how people learn from failure and success by observing competitors' mistakes on a computer. Brain imaging showed that the players in the study were less likely to repeat the same mistakes made by the competitors. The competitor's failures generated additional neuron activity in the player's brain. That's stimulating to me — and proof that shortcuts can be favorable and not indicative of misbehavior or trouble.

Highly successful people use some form of time-saving methods. There are so many shortcuts available to you if you use your imagination to find and read about them. Recently, I shared a very simple shortcut for a weekly conference call with colleagues. I noticed many of them were wasting their time dialing the exact same phone number and writing down the exact same access code to dial into their mobile phones every week to get on a routine call. I researched the company's internal website and found that the company provided a free app on the internal portal that was downloadable and programmable to any set of dial-ins and access codes. If these employees had looked for a shortcut, they would have saved both time and money for the company.

Being efficient has huge payoffs. When you have a repetitive task, there are shortcuts available to dramatically reduce wasted time. If you routinely use any type of computers or software, there are awesome shortcuts for ALL OF THEM that will change your life. Find them and learn them. Many people are missing out on endless shortcuts for using the internet. Read as much as you can about new technologies; it takes work up front to search, but the more time you invest clearing unnecessary steps, the more time you can spend with your family, and the more valuable you become at work and business.

shortcuts are not your enemy

Another shortcut to success is turning off the television — record your favorite shows and watch them commercial free when you need a break. Watching television is entertaining and can be a good distraction, if not overly done. Cable and

broadcast networks average 13-15 minutes of commercials in a sixty-minute show. We are getting pounded with 15-30 second commercial spots in between our five to six minutes of enjoying The Walking Dead. I favor cable type programs myself. If you are a road warrior and listen to talk radio, you've noticed advertisements have been built-in to the host to keep an audience from tuning out. Certain radio stations can have up to twenty minutes of commercials and promos in an hour. I use my satellite radio to pause and fast-forward radio shows, so I can listen selectively. That's worth the price of the monthly membership. There's way too much communication and clutter in our lives, so use shortcuts to remove them. We have better things to do like work on our dreams!

Never stop learning, and never be afraid to share what you've learned. People can benefit from your experience and guidance. Not everyone is as intuitive as you are and may not ever have the opportunities you have. Another wonderful shortcut to real success is to help others get what they desire in life, and in the process, you'll get everything you wish for. I learned that from Zig Ziglar. Many doors have opened for me because of helping hands. At the same time, I've opened doors for many. I've always done that since I was young. A number of my teenage friends had jobs growing up because business owners I delivered to asked me if I knew of someone to help grow their business — they trusted me and my work.

Another effective strategy is to use the magic word NO. That one word alone can unleash your success.

You can say...

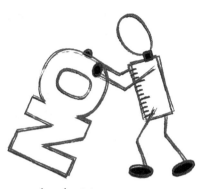

NO to too much television

NO to time-wasting habits

NO to complaining

NO to unproductive meetings

NO to waiting for the perfect time — there's never a perfect time for anything

NO to multitasking, unless you are commuting and reading or listening to a productive book

NO to disorganization

NO to failing to delegate to others

There are so many time-suckers trying to gain our attention. Identify them and kick them to the curb. There's a distinct difference between "busy work" and "getting results work." Productive people are very selective with their YES. One last thing I would like to share about good shortcuts is this: anything big you are trying to achieve will take time and will require everything you've got. Time is your most valuable asset; it's more valuable than money. You can replace money, but when time is spent, it is gone forever. The most important things you can do to help create happiness and satisfaction is to gain control of your time and how it's being spent. To reclaim some time is to

plan ahead and find certain time-saving strategies that work for you — which are also known as shortcuts.

Some things in life are so simplistic that they stand the test of time. Over twenty years ago, I embraced an incredibly simple method that was taught to the legendary businessman, Charles Schwab, and it's worked marvelously for me. Since majoring in industrial design at A&D and researching the industrial revolution, I've always been fascinated by Charles Schwab and Andrew Carnegie, and want- ed to learn everything I could about them. This includes their Principles of Success; the use of Vertical Integration; and The Gospel of Wealth. Both men came from poverty and worked their way up to become a "super structure" example of success; they also contributed tremendously to society with their incredible wealth. We can all thank An- drew Carnegie for the public libraries many of us visit. The next time you enter a large building that shows some of the overhead steel structures, you may notice a steel beam on the ceiling that looks like the letter H. It was created by a steel company lead by the late Charles Schwab in the early 1900's, and it became the standard in building skyscrapers and bridges because of its amazing strength and fireproof ability.

As legend has it, Charles Schwab was trying to find more efficient ways to increase the effectiveness of himself and his people and met a gentleman named Ivy Lee. Before finishing a day's work, Lee taught the executives to create a list of the six most important things to get done the next day: each day, begin with the first item on the list, and do not move onto the next until that one task is done. Keep moving down the list until each goal is achieved. If an item was not completed that particular day, it moved to the next day's list. Repeat the process every day.

"Don't worry if you don't complete everything on the schedule. At least you will have completed the most important projects before getting to the less important ones," said Lee.

Schwab hired him as an advisor and compensated him with $25,000 for that one idea, around 1918. How much is that worth in today's dollars? How much could this one tip be worth to you tomorrow? Lee is also considered the father of modern public relations; he served as the publicity director for the American Red Cross during WWI, an organization I have much admiration for being on the receiving and giving end of the spectrum, as I mentioned in a previous chapter.

What am I saying? Results-oriented people make time for what is important and stay focused. Busy people make time for anything and everything. I've learned the hard way that "A" for effort doesn't keep the lights on or keep you in your home or your car. I've met and worked with very busy people that were highly unproductive. My question is: what results are you seeing with your efforts? Are you trying hard and not getting ahead? It doesn't take much to turn results around with the right priorities and right focus.

join the league and get "Ivy Lee" focused

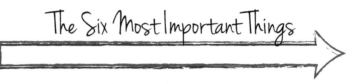

The Six Most Important Things

a. each night, make a list of the top 6 things you want to accomplish tomorrow — prioritize this in order of importance.

b. each day, start with the first task and keep working on it until it's completed — do not move onto the next task until done.

c. if any tasks were left at the end of the day, move them over to the top of the tomorrow's list — if you only complete tasks 1-4 today, tasks 5-6 will become your first tasks 1-2 tomorrow.

1. _____

2. _____

3. _____

4. _____

5. _____

6. _____

NOTES
I am just one simple idea away

CINCH IT #8

I'M SELLING
YOU'RE SELLING
EVERYONE'S SELLING

"Everyone lives by selling something."
– Robert Louis Stevenson

I n late 2006, I was introduced to a terrific job opportunity with a company that sells leading products in over 175 countries. I was envisioning this as a long-term career option. After a lengthy interview process, including a variety of assessments, I was offered the position and was very excited to accept it. There were times in the interview process I thought they were going to ask for my first-born child; it was similar to applying for a big mortgage when they asked for previous years of W2 forms for income verification.

I said, "Sure, I would be delighted to share my income history with you. May I ask first, are you considering making an offer?"

The internal company recruiter replied, "I believe they are."

I obviously provided what they required to make an offer. It was an awesome opportunity for me to work in a specialty consultant capacity across a large region. I was hired to support the medical supply team to grow the medical device portion of the business since they had a vast supply portfolio and limited device experience. I worked in the field with a senior director I had interviewed with, and we both had an enjoyable conversation regarding the interview process.

"That was an exceedingly thorough interview process," I said.

He responded, "It's vital to hire the best people." "Thank you for that," I said.

"We had an incredible talent pool that applied, and that made it difficult for us to decide," he said.

I felt humbled and asked, "What lead you to your decision?"

"You have an impressive resume, and we wanted to get to know the person behind the paper," he said.

I replied, "This organization has a remarkable history, and it was equally important for me to interview you so I could make the right choice for myself and my family."

"You also have a phenomenal attitude. I was selling; you were selling, everyone was selling," he said.

That particular statement stuck with me because it's meaningful and relevant to everyone. If you happen to be a professional salesperson, I would expect that you believe it's the most wonderful thing to do for a living. Let's face it; nothing happens until a sale is made. Whether you are in a sales capacity or not, you are always selling. You may be selling your friend to go on a date; you may be selling your church congregation to participate on a mission trip; you may be selling your manager on a promotion; you may be selling your patients on why they should be compliant with a certain therapy, or you may be selling a college admissions team. Everyone is always selling themselves or their ideas, and if you're a not, then you are not growing. I know there are people out there that have a poor impression of salespeople. Benjamin Franklin said it best: "The rotten apple spoils the companion." Because of a few bad apples, the rest get labeled. Professional salespeople do not fall in this category. Did you know that excellent sales professionals are the highest paid employees? They rank up there with lawyer and physician compensation, and more often than not, have a better-balanced home life. That's good company to be in, if you ask me.

expect the unexpected

I once sold a unique breathing tube that was designed specifically for the pediatric anatomy, ranging from a tiny newborn to a school-age child. As I began to introduce this new product to hospitals, the clinicians recognized the value of the device, especially within their tiniest patient population with injuries or trauma in the neck area. A child's trachea is very fragile, and no person wants to cause damage. If a person can't breathe on their own, they are attached to a ventilator or breathing machine, much like the one my mom was on. A tube is placed in the windpipe

or trachea to create an airway or pathway. When people go into certain surgeries or are hit with trauma, they may need a similar type tube.

While I began to get this device into the hospitals, the company was made aware of an issue, and they voluntarily recalled the product off the market for safety reasons. Consumer safety is the highest priority. This scenario can and does happen to all industries. In fact, I've been through this process multiple times with several product categories. The unexpected happens. You can't avoid it. You need to be prepared for it. Imagine all of the resources, testing, effort, time and expense involved behind the scenes to get a product approved and placed in the market. It's enormous. Countless hours, and sometimes years, are spent creating processes: building, manufacturing, delivering presentations, training, etc. However, all of that can shut down in an instant. It's crucial to be self-sufficient and to have good thinking and problem-solving skills to help a client through a process like this internally and externally. It builds trust. That's the colossal value you bring. This is why we go through an exhaustive interview process with an organization. What matters in business is your ability to help.

change is constant

Industries, companies and markets always change. I constantly try to find new ways of improving myself, so I can bring more value to my clients, both internal and external. Internal clients are the people you work with inside the organization. External clients are the people you serve outside the organization; the ones that pay to keep the lights on. When I read something of interest or observe something of value, I'll share it with the appropriate people. I've always done this throughout my military and professional career. Key people eventually recognize that, and you begin to develop a reputation for excellence. Good fortune usually follows. There was a time I was invited to attend a very high-level meeting regarding a divisional reorganization in the company related to sales and operations planning. I was the only field-based representative invited to the meeting along with the executive leadership team and learned how these decisions are made from an inside perspective.

Organizations reorganize or restructure for a variety of reasons. Some major reasons are to improve results, profits and efficiencies. You may see this when a new leader takes the helm or when the organization changes ownership. It can happen for many reasons, and it always happens. Make no mistake about it; change always comes. Strategies get realigned, and people do as well. Some make the cut, some don't, for a variety of reasons. In this particular case, the goal was to develop key strategies and tactics to create a more specialized and highly focused sales team to deliver better results. The successful organizations improve the business's ability to handle the most important decisions.

The point of this story is this: business and life are unpredictable and are always progressing. Everything you've worked hard for can unravel quickly beyond your control. Just the thought of this type of uncertainty can trigger anxiety and fear for many. Regrettably, many people are not prepared to handle it. Preparation is key here so you can bounce back from a setback like this quickly. It's not about *if* it will happen, but *when*. I can't stress this point enough. The best of the best loses at times.

For example, I've been ranked a number one and number two sales professional with a company and was let go during an acquisition. The company that acquired us was originally established back when Theodore Roosevelt was President of the United States, and Andrew Carnegie start- ed the Carnegie Institute for Science in Washington DC. This particular organization already had multiple representatives in my area with much longer tenure. Being armed and prepared with the right information is half the battle. Never feel trapped in anything you do; options are avail- able. Know that there is always room at the table for your skills and attitude somewhere. Never, ever, stop striving for you and your family! I have written out some questions to ponder on to get the process started.

    a. write about the most significant accomplishment in your life

    b. what's been the most stressful situation you've ever found yourself in at work or home? what did you do?

    c. how did it impact your (company, family, business, command)?

    d. what are you most proud of?

    e. what steps do you follow to analyze a problem before taking action?

    f. have you ever been dissatisfied at work? what did you do improve on it? what didn't you do?

    g. think about a goal you've reached. how did you achieve it?

    h. if a goal was not reached, why haven't you achieved it yet?

    i. how well do you listen to people? do you listen for a response or do you listen to understand?

    j. how do you relate to people? can you share a relevant story? if not, can you borrow a friend or co-worker's story and relate?

IT'S A CINCH

HOW TO PREPARE FOR CHANGE
AT WORK AND HOME

a. the first thing to do is develop unshakeable self-esteem — this goes back to trusting thyself; know that you are on the planet to do something special; there are things you know how to do better than anyone else; reflect on the accomplishments you've had over your lifetime; when you really think about it, you've made a significant difference in someone's life, and that's special!

b. second, always have a learning activity in place — if it's necessary to improve interview skills, or focus on communication, there's an effective story telling process called STAR, which stands for Situation, Task, Action and Result; practice communicating in this format; it will serve you well.

c. third, find a need and make a contribution — it will help you communicate and actively be part of a group; identify the "why" behind the need and great progress can be made; you will become a valuable asset to your network or group!

NOTES
I am just one simple idea away

CINCH IT #9

DEFY LOGIC AND MAJOR IN SOME MINOR THINGS

"I see great things in baseball"
– Walt Whitman

Not long ago, I was working closely with a particular pediatric surgeon at a teaching hospital located in North Carolina. He was demonstrating a minimally invasive surgical procedure to final year medical students in the operating room. At the time, I sold a medical device that reduced surgical steps requiring fewer incisions while placing a feeding tube in a baby or child. This was a great solution for him, and he wanted to try it because it lowered risk for complications that other procedures may pose.

"Bob, the locker room is around the corner, get scrubbed up and I'll see you in the O.R. suite," the surgeon said.

"I'll be right there Doctor," I replied.

As I entered the O.R., the surgeon explained to his team, "This is a new product and technique for me, and I want to fully understand its clinical advantages. For safety, we are going to use simultaneous laparoscopic and endoscopic guidance for this procedure. It's important for us to see outside the stomach wall with my laparoscope and in- side the stomach with my endoscope to confirm placement of the introducer needle and feeding tube."

"Thank you, Doctor," I said, while he began to review the anatomy of the patient and verify the patient's identity.

"Pause/Time-Out," the doctor said.

All the members of the operating team verbally verified that their understanding matches the patient's identity and procedure. The surgical team in the operating room was made up of the surgeon, the anesthesiologist, the circulating nurse — which helps the surgeon during the procedure, the surgical tech, two medical students, and me.

The patient was fully draped and protected, with the exception of the surgical site, and the patient's skin was washed with solution to kill the germs normally found on the skin.

"Batter up, Bob," the surgeon said to me. "What do you mean by batter up?" I asked.

The surgeon positioned himself on the left side of the patient and looked at the two monitors facing him. He turned to me and pointed out the four marks in the shape of a diamond on the patient's exposed skin where the feeding tube would be placed.

"I will be using the baseball diamond concept for the laparoscopic portion... Camera is home plate, right port is first base, center port is second base, and left port is third base," the physician said.

"I easily understood that," I thought.

The assistant was located beside the surgeon; the anesthesiologist was at the head of the bed; the circulating nurse was nearby monitoring and coordinating the activities in the suite; and the instrument scrub nurse was located at the foot of the bed. The actual placement of the feeding tube took the least amount of time during this process.

"Bob, we're ready to use your device: walk me through the process one more time," the doctor said.

The doctor and I practiced the steps before the actual procedure. Pre-planning and practice are key factors to favorable outcomes. During the procedure, I clearly explained the steps, and he went through the procedure with great ease like a well-oiled machine (more on that later), and the patient benefited. Even while having written policies and procedures in place, healthcare systems still have flaws and create medical errors.

Process expertise is important to help any organization be successful, and that requires an understanding of four basic teamwork competencies, which are similarly used in patient care. The same principle can be applied at home *and* work.

a. communication — communicate with influence
b. leadership — lead by example
c. mutual support — shared decision making

d. situation monitoring — actively scan and access things around you to gain information and understanding to support the family or team.

Since this surgeon shared a baseball diamond analogy and I love baseball, I'll keep with the same theme. Professional baseball is made up of major league and minor league teams and players. Majoring in the minors, in this context, means to focus on those small, crucial, fundamental skills that will elevate you to major league status. This may come as a surprise to some, but minor league teams play with the same rule book as the major league. If they play with the same rules, then what differentiates them? Drum roll please, the value each player brings to the team, meaning their skill and contribution.

I get the following question frequently, "How can I break into that field or this industry?" The very best way to get noticed in anything you desire is to try it out and perform at your best. That could be as a volunteer for the time being. There are many careers that are skill specific for advancement and require a great deal of practice. Practice makes that possible. For example, the very best sales professionals practice their craft routinely and bring tremendous value to their clients. Find a way to always practice with the best people you can find — people who have greater skill sets than you. You will get noticed being around top performers because top performers draw attention and you'll automatically benefit from that attention. You don't need to be number one to get noticed. You just need to be better than good, and things will happen for you.

Some people associate a "time-out" with correcting behavioral problems and being put in isolation, such as a child being put in a corner to think about what they've done wrong. As a parent, I've always thought that particular discipline technique wasn't effective. As a business and medical consultant, I think time-outs are very effective, especially after personally observing hundreds of surgical cases in hospitals. This technique was implemented to prevent wrong-site, wrong-anatomy, wrong-procedure or wrong-person surgeries. In addition, as people are becoming more resistant to antibiotics, antibiotic stewardship programs in hospitals are also utilizing an anti-biotic time-out strategy to review appropriate antibiotics used. A 2014 Centers for Disease Control report found 30- 50% of all antibiotics prescribed in U.S. acute care hospitals might be incorrect.[9]

I really appreciate the awareness and focus a time-out can bring to a patient's safety. Applying a similar time-out technique at home *and* work can be very productive as you are running around trying to get everything done faster and faster. It could be used as a practical check list. It will increase thinking, speaking and listening skills. It could help reinforce good habits over bad habits. Time-outs can reduce anger and stress. It could save you a great deal of time and heartache by identifying risks. A carpenter is trained to measure twice and cut once. Coaches and players are permitted time-outs on the field to regroup and assess a critical play or situation.

take a time-out once in a while

One summer day I was at a New York Mets baseball game with my entire firehouse from Long Island. We had a neighboring fire department run standby for us so we could all attend as a group. As I focused on the players on the

field, I saw one of the guys from my group jump over several rows of seats to my right side. My first thought was that a fight broke out — sometimes a fan can get out of line when passion and beers collide. I looked over to see people moving from the seats, and the guy from my firehouse bearhugs a woman from behind to help her from choking. I watched closely for a few seconds — enough to see that it wasn't working for him. He was also a career firefighter in the city. Whatever she was choking on wasn't dislodging. I immediately climbed over to them and tapped my buddy on the shoulder to move aside. I gently wrapped my arm around her waist and placed my fist above the navel with my thumb against the abdomen. I whispered to her, "relax — stay calm," then gave her a quick inward abdominal thrust and the hot dog shot out like a rocket. She coughed for a brief moment and took a deep breath, then turned around and gave me the biggest hug and said, "Thank You!"

I looked at her and said, "I trained for this moment for years!" She sat back down in her seat as if nothing happened. That's a true Mets fan!

I love everything about baseball; it's a lot like life, where we always have a chance to make a comeback anytime in the game, including the final inning with two outs and two strikes against us!

Batter-up. Proper choke of the baseball bat and effective swing. Walk off, home run!

BOOM!

IT'S A CINCH

IT PAYS TO PLAY AT WORK AND HOME

a. take the group to a baseball game — minor leagues are great

b. have a CPR and First Aid training at work *and* home

c. dancing is fun — take dancing lessons as a group

d. group cooking class — you may learn new skills to use at home

e. celebrate holidays at work *and* home

f. success and recognition — celebrate with fun foods

g. have a talent show at work *and* home

h. bring in a photographer to take fun pictures

i. hire a clean comedian to do a mock speech and make fun

j. go to a museum with the group at work *and* home

k. go to the public library as a group and research a new project

l. utilize the corporate conference room for a movie night

m. join a bowling league at work *and* home

n. have a carnival at work *and* home — size doesn't matter

o. have a "bring the kids to work day" — take them on a tour and learn

p. take a unique behind the scenes zoo tour with the group

q. provide a game area to relax at work *and* home

r. create a "take your dog to work day"
s. celebrate your baptism day — reinvent yourself.

NOTES
I am just one simple idea away

SECTION FOUR:

DEMONSTRATION

CINCH IT #10

TRUST THYSELF

"Trust yourself. Create the kind of self that you will be happy to live with all your life."
– Golda Meir

I was recently asked by a colleague, "Why do you think more people fail than succeed?"

That's a great question!

I believe it has to do with mindset and attitude. People don't trust themselves and give up too soon.

Orison Swett Marden wrote a book called Pushing to the Front, with an original print in 1894. It's been said that it is doubtful any other book, other than the Bible, has been the turning point in more lives. Marden said, "Discouragement, fear, doubt, lack of self-confidence, are

germs which have killed the prosperity and happiness of thousands of people." How and what we think of ourselves is critically important. It's a matter of what's going on inside your own head. If you are not in the right frame of mind, the skills you learn can only take you so far. You have to have a high level of mental toughness in today's competitive climate.

I've been through a myriad of formal corporate programs including a series of sales methodologies, coaching and leadership programs, accountability and negotiating training with Fortune 500 and Fortune 1000 companies. Unfortunately, almost every single one of these trainings missed the boat when it came to developing an individual's mindset, including working on building self-confidence. Most programs were mainly focused on developing skills, and the return on investment was very small from my vantage point.

During the trainings I attended, participants were typically expected to provide candid feedback without fear of retribution or punishment after each program. I've always provided thoughtful feedback, making sure I highlighted both the positive things the training's done and the areas we can improve. As organizations implement a culture of accountability, teams are encouraged to share feedback to help the organization improve; but I noticed not many people actually share critical feedback because they fear saying too much, so they fly under the radar and go unnoticed. Just the word accountability sends shivers down someone's spine. It's important to understand the corporate culture in any organization so you can properly set the stage as it relates to giving balanced feedback.

For example, I attended a leadership development program for a very well-known company and the material was not well executed by the consultant. In fact, all the managers in attendance recognized it wasn't going well about a quarter of the way into the training, and many suggested to leadership to shorten the schedule because it wasn't providing value. Everyone in the room agreed, including the senior leadership folks. As the program abruptly concluded, the evaluation forms were handed out to everyone in the room. For each question, we had an option to circle one of five impressions of that program from: Strongly Agree; Agree; Neutral; Disagree, and Strongly Disagree. The form contained about a dozen basic questions about the program such as: the training met my expectations; I will be able to apply the knowledge learned; the quality of the instructor was good; what aspects of the training could be improved, etc. The forms were collected and reviewed during the short break.

As the meeting kicked off again, the corporate training manager mentioned he reviewed the evaluations and was confused about the responses from people. He was wondering why nearly all of the managers in the room selected favorable impressions of the program, when that clearly wasn't the case. He also pointed out that all but two individuals in the room did not share any written comments regarding what aspects of the training could be improved upon (and I was one of the two that did). This was contradictory. Were the managers being sensitive to the consultant, knowing they may never see him again; or were they not willing to share what they really thought of the program for fear of speaking out? I found that fascinating.

It's crucial to build upon a solid foundation of self-trust and self-confidence within your own mind to make a significant contribution at work *and* home. That's what superior performing people do. If you wholeheartedly like and trust yourself, you'll be able to create an amazing lifestyle. For example, when I was working forty-five-hour weeks and going to college full-time in the city, I typically commuted on the city subway system. Occasionally, I would splurge and take the more expensive Long Island Railroad home, although it was only for two brief stations. I did that so I could act the part of being a professional businessman. I felt a sense of accomplishment sitting on a comfortable train, surrounding myself with people in their business attire. This simple act gave me a sense of self-confidence in business. I also dreamed of one day buying a home on Long Island for my family taking the same line and made that a reality with consistent thought. The subway didn't have that appeal whatsoever. It was always hustle and bustle on the subway system.

Another way to build self-confidence is by always thinking and acting positively. I am known for my positive energy. When someone asks how I am doing, I respond with, "I'm doing better than good, how about yourself?" Then I usually get a response back from someone saying, "Wow! Must be great to feel that way." I also like to say things are going swimmingly, since my last name is Poole. This attitude of gratitude led me to meet dynamic people at the Dale Carnegie® Training Center in New York, and join what Napoleon Hill referred as a Mastermind Group called Goal Getters Group, started by a wonderful Dale Carnegie friend. Napoleon Hill wrote the landmark book *Think and Grow Rich*. While at Dale Carnegie, I've participated in over 100 hours of various training programs as an assistant, including the Dale Carnegie® Instructors Conference. That's a sure-fire way to build self-confidence.

IT'S A CINCH

TAKE RESPONSIBILITY AT WORK AND HOME

a. trust yourself — believe you'll win and you will
b. think — see the big picture in new ways and create ideas
c. compete with yourself, not others — know yourself well
d. plan and take action — enjoy the scenic route once in a while
e. what gets measured, gets learned — most else is forgotten
f. identify your unique talents and take pride in them
g. be prepared — preparation seems to be a common theme
h. accomplish something — quick way to build self-confidence
i. dress for success — it works
j. take a chance at something and give it your best
k. graciously receive from others — enjoy the compliment or gift
l. give praise — people love to help and they want to help
m. stand up for what you believe in — understand your worth
n. know you have choices — you are never stuck
o. have a written schedule — keep your commitments

p. participate in training programs — training companies use volunteer audiences for new practicing trainers to speak to.

NOTES
I am just one simple idea away

CINCH IT #11

MAKE A DIFFERENCE

*"The purpose of life is not to be happy. It is to be useful,
to be honorable, to be compassionate, to have it make
some difference that you have lived and lived well."*
– Ralph Waldo Emerson

Working in any marketplace is increasingly challenging, and bringing value is more important than ever to compete and succeed. A short time ago, I was involved in a hostile bid against two competitors within a huge health system. The hospital system invited each company separately to present respective solutions. The competitors and I offered very similar products, although we were the first to market with a simplistic device; an end-cap filled with alcohol to protect a patient's injection port from bloodstream infections.

From the start, I had a feeling this was going to be a tough negotiation. The moment I arrived for my presentation, I was immediately told by the clinical coordinator leading the meeting that they only had a short amount of time to meet.

"Full disclosure: we are inviting you and two other companies to review product options," the leader told me. "We prefer to do a six-month trial to gather enough data to make a choice, along with a possible clinical study," he continued.

"Thank you for sharing that. May I ask you some specifics about the project?" I asked.

"I would like to know how much your device will cost?" he said.

"I understand, we'll be sure to cover that today. I just have a few questions, so I can fully understand your needs and expectations. Would you be kind enough to define the problem you are experiencing?" I responded.

He provided some feedback, and then I asked a follow-up question. "What steps have your clinical teams taken to solve the problem on their own? Why do you think the problem is occurring?"

They spent about ten minutes sharing the hospital's practice and policies, and then I asked, "What are your expectations and objectives for a six-month trial?"

After I asked several thoughtful, pre-planned questions and listened to their purpose for this change, the meeting warmed up completely. They realized I was genuinely interested in getting to the root cause of the issues they were experiencing. I asked additional questions and learned about their goals and addressed them. The beginning of the meeting was strictly slated for 20-30 minutes, as I was warned when I arrived, but we were together discussing the project for 90 minutes. When you are dealing with people in general, you need to have great flexibility. Toward the end of the conversation, I brought the pricing question back up, since it was one of their first questions.

"I would like to address your pricing question, if I may?" I proposed.

"The cost is critical to this deal," the supply chain director replied.

"Cost is very important. We are not the lowest cost provider for this product," I said. "I know you will be receiving a lower price from our competitors, since they are trying to gain market share," I continued while sharing the price in writing.

"If you want to have a dog in this hunt, you have to give this system a better price," the supply chain director said.

"It's more complex than price alone," I replied.

"Tell us, why should we use your product over the others?" the clinical leader asked.

"I'm glad you asked that question. The device is a great tool, but we don't just sell a product and leave you to deal with the problems. Here's where we differ; my organization provides a turnkey process that is all-inclusive in the price. Let me explain."

At this point in the conversation, I provided detailed strategies and tactics they can implement to show how we can meet and exceed the explicit goals they shared. I shared several key findings behind the successes we've had with clients similar in size and scope of their respective environment, and outlined a process for them to follow. I also created a cost analysis, including three different scenarios they may consider, clearly showing what the

device would likely cost the system upfront, and what the anticipated infection reduction and savings could yield if they followed the process. Several weeks after that meeting, I received a call that I was awarded the deal, and it was not for a six-month trial; it was immediate and for the entire health system. That felt terrific.

Here's the thing to consider. You will win some, and you will lose some. Size up the opportunity you are interested in. Is the relationship or business worth your valuable time and effort? Making a difference is time-consuming, and there are no guarantees you'll ever be rewarded for your efforts. As a golden rule, it's best practice to always be pro-active in preparing important information and thoughtful questions when someone or an organization agrees to meet with you. I've been involved in thousands of sales meetings over the years, and many times, only had one shot to get it right — so preparation is paramount.

Recently, I lost an opportunity to a competitor because they offered a drastically lower price for their device. There are times when you need to walk away from a deal that can hurt you; this pertains to both home and business. A few months after losing this particular deal, I received a call from the client asking to switch to my organization, since they experienced a problem the other company couldn't solve. The best prepared doesn't always get the deal, but it's the best way to conduct yourself. Serve with excellence in everything you do.

focus on the "vital few" that make a difference

You are probably familiar with the Pareto Principle (also known as the 80/20 rule). Economist Vilfredo Pareto developed the principle by observing peapods in his garden where 20% of the peapods contained 80% of the peas. There's been a great deal of research and books written around this principle since Pareto published his first paper when Benjamin Harrison was President of the United States. The Pareto Principle applies to many things in business and life. In business, 80% of my sales come from 20% of my clients, for example. The major point is that we want to focus on the smaller number of things that bring the most value to our lives.

159

IT'S A CINCH

MAKE A DIFFERENCE AT WORK AND HOME

a. begin at home with your own family — ask "how was your day?"
b. commit to continually better yourself
c. mentor someone and share your knowledge
d. realize the impact you are already making in someone's life
e. start a goal getters group or a think tank group
f. clean up after yourself — leave a place better than the way you found it
g. give someone a heartfelt compliment
h. recognize accomplishments — people love recognition
i. take time today to hold a door open for others
j. ask a knowledgeable person for their insight
k. encourage someone — stay away from gossip
l. develop a list of good questions to use in a conversation
m. listen well — make an extra effort to learn about a person
n. donate — volunteer
o. let someone know how much they mean to you
p. learn someone's name and use it in conversation with them

NOTES
I am just one simple idea away

CINCH IT #12

GET THE WHEELS TURNING

"The squeaky wheel may get the most oil,
but it's also the first to be replaced."
– Marilyn vos Savant

For the past nineteen years, I've been intensely focused on acute care in hospitals from neonatal to adults. Along the way, I have met people who have solved complex clinical problems with unbelievably simple solutions, purely because they were observant and intuitive. For example, this little thing called hypothermia can be very problematic in surgery. Patients may get too cold during surgery because of the cool environment, and the blood and intravenous fluids delivered to them are room temperature by the time it enters their bloodstream — which is actually enough to drop their core body temperature. I've actually

seen a patient under anesthesia shiver on the operating table like a fish flip-flopping out of water because of perioperative hypothermia.

Like many other inventions, all it took was for someone to observe a huge problem and think of a simple way to solve it. In this case, the inventors designed a way to deliver fluids into the bloodstream at 98.6 degrees via a heated water "jacket" that covers the inner fluid path. The tube was designed to have two outer lumens for the warm water bath to circulate and heat the center lumen where the blood and fluid flow. What's interesting about this design is it's actually the reverse concept of marine engines that power boats and ships. The cool seawater is used to "jacket" or cool the hot oil the engines produce. I wish I had thought of it, since I worked on those very engines in the U.S. Navy. The marketing around that simple idea was brilliant as well: the company used a photo of a snow monkey bathing in the hot springs of a snowcapped mountain in Japan. What an image!

we are all problem solvers

During the past four years, I've had a devotion to help reduce a little-known problem called hospital-acquired infections (HAIs). I met wonderful people in this specialized area, and it has since grown into a passion for me. According to the Centers for Disease Control and Prevention, each year, about 1 in 25 U.S. hospital patients is diagnosed with at least one infection related to hospital care alone.[9] There was a time, not so long ago, that medical providers considered HAIs were an inevitable result of delivering care to patients. Based on a variety of reasons, HAIs are now considered unacceptable and largely preventable. It really was the squeaky wheel that got the oil when hospitals stopped getting reimbursed for mistakes and infections they created. Since these infections are not considered an epidemic, they are not broadcast in the local news and are generally out of sight from the public. It's important for all of us to understand that not all antibiotics can cure your hospital infection, especially since strains of bacteria called "superbugs" are becoming resistant to our most powerful drugs. For example, an organism called Staphylococcus Aureus is normal skin flora found on about one-third of individuals, and seems to cause no harm — unless an environment is created for it to thrive, such as in hospitals where this bacteria can get into the bloodstream — and that can be fatal.[9] Despite the years of elevated attention given by state and federal government agencies, health organizations and hospitals, improvements and measures continue to be necessary since mistakes and infections in hospitals ensue, although at a much lower rate. When you are dealing with people-dependency or human factor, mistakes are always going to be present.

There are two key takeaways here; what you don't know could hurt you, and there is always room at the table to improve a process, regardless of how much attention it's given. That's where you can help. It only takes one simple idea to develop a game-changer for an industry or to help in your own home. You are just one idea away to greatness.

lubricate your ideas and skills

The concept of a well-oiled machine is to operate with efficiency by minimizing friction for easy movement. In

the U.S. Navy and the Fire & EMS service, I made it a habit to take the extra small steps to ensure the equipment was always at peak readiness; more so than most. It's the little details that go a long, long way and make the biggest impact. This simple "lubricating" philosophy has enabled me to serve my clients very well by figuring out ways to get things moving easier for them. The financial savings in hospitals related to the infection prevention initiatives I helped implement is valued in the millions. It is feasible that someone reading this book was helped by one of the very devices I marketed over the years. According to the Journal of American Medical Association, despite the massive quality improvement initiatives by hospitals, an estimated $9.8 billion is spent each year treating five major HAIs nationwide.[10]

a new normal is required

Developing a new normal is necessary to achieve big breakthroughs. I would encourage you to involve key people in the process for optimal success. Shared ideas are always more powerful than going at it alone. Here's a way to think about this: in a hospital, a patient (think in the context of a friend or family member) may not be in a normal, clear-minded state for a host of reasons, and they could benefit from an advocate by their side to help with information. I've been in just about every area of a hospital where patients did not have a family member or person with them to support them. It's sad to see that. Don't be that person. Some of us put our entire trust and care in the hands of others, especially when we are most vulnerable, and even with the best intentions and painstaking care, terrible mistakes happen. Everyone should play a key role at work *and* home. There is greater strength in numbers, so include people in your ideas.

How do we maximize that? Utilize a simple six-step activity to deliver game-changing outcomes. This process made me very successful, and I believe it can do the same for you. Simply **fill in the blanks** with your respective audience and make it a CINCH.

- become the ultimate (**example**: patient) advocate — *a strong desire*
- learn the (**example**: hospital's) modus operandi and identify variations in practice or methods — *find the how and why things are done*
- identify key partners to gain different perspectives and insight
- introduce appropriate solutions for results — *solve a problem*
- implement and communicate without fail — *inform and share*
- measure for results and make necessary adjustments — *what gets measured, gets results.*

It's a win-win-win strategy for both the home *and* work.

I have some great news — you don't need to figure it all out at once. Start small and take it inch-by-inch. All you need to do TODAY is envision your endgame and get started. That's the most critical step. Once you start the journey, the answers will begin to unfold as you steamroll your fears and objections. As you begin to gain traction, you'll find that your ideas and achievements will attract attention. This

may lead to some opposition and competition, and you may feel uncomfortable at first, but it's a vital part of the process, so embrace it. This stuff has a way of working itself out. It's really amazing how simply this process works. As you unleash your powerful mind, you'll begin to illuminate and spot things that were always present but couldn't be seen before.

IT'S A CINCH

HOW TO BECOME A WELL-OILED MACHINE

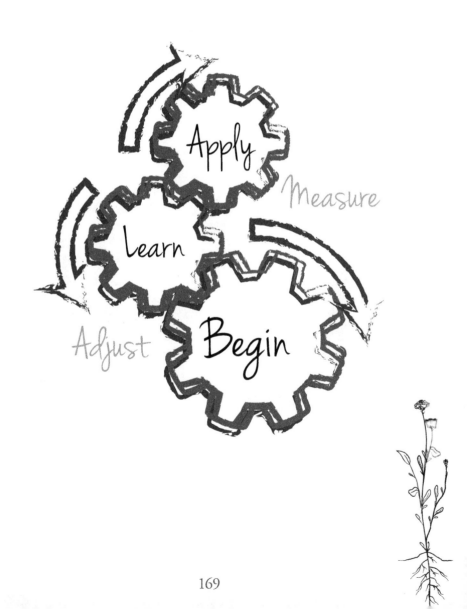

NOTES
I am just one simple idea away

SECTION FIVE:
ENCHANTMENT

CONCLUSION

BEE THAT ONE

"It takes a bee to get the honey out."
– Arthur Guiterman

We are coming to the end here, but it's actually just the beginning of a fresh start. It's my hope that you are inspired to bloom where you are planted at this very moment. My friend, it really doesn't matter the place you're beginning from, or what's happened previously. What matters is where you are headed. I've learned to embrace something called a "Survivor's High." There's never been a better time in history to take a chance and live on your own terms. During my travels in healthcare, the military community, and emergency services, I've met some incredible people who survived a terrible trauma or a debilitating illness — and observed first-hand the most amazing zest they had for life. These individuals understood how precious life and opportunities are better than anyone. Many have a knack for finding good in the bad. I believe I am one of them, and I have a feeling you are as well.

It's time to create a new buzz in life. An effective way to get excited and get behind something is to think about what actually gets you going each day without the need for an alarm. I trust my body clock. I look forward to getting up every day to see what new opportunities await me. I rarely ever need an alarm clock. Once in a while, I'll set one because of a late night, but I'm always up before it buzzes, like clockwork! Another effective way to discover what you like to do is through body language. Our bodies make a lot of unconscious responses to different situations. For example, when I'm happy and excited, I find myself looking up often. I also find that I walk with a spring in my step when I am happy and confident. Body language can reveal a lot when you learn and pay attention to it.

One of the foundational parts needed to unleash potential is to identify key strengths and possible weaknesses and take immediate action to build on them. A rock-solid foundation is key to sustainable load-balancing. Once I truly understood this part, I became amazingly productive in all areas of my life. Let's take balancing cues from mother nature and consider honey bees for a moment, since they are highly social and are responsible for the unlimited harvest we enjoy. Also, honey bees have an extensive track record on earth; they've been around for millions of years. We should be able to learn a thing or two from these survivors. I happen to be great friends with a beekeeper who harvests amazing honey. It's pure gold.

bee a pollinator

As we all were taught in grade school, pollinators fertilize plants to make fruit and seeds, and bees are among the finest at this. Without pollinators, certain fruits won't grow. Much the same, if you don't "pollinate" your ideas, they won't grow either. The pollinator must have contact with the flowers to fertilize. Bees get their nectar and pollen from the flower while landing on them. Simply put, no bees; no contact; no berries. Every business and family need a pollinator to cross-pollinate ideas and emotions by touching the mind and heart of another; when they touch another, the ideas and emotions begin to be fruitful. Fundamentally, it's a natural process — so behave naturally.

bee attractive

Win with a grin. Have you ever walked down the street and randomly smiled at a person walking in your direction and they smiled back? I tend to be a very happy and content person and smile often. I'm not referring to the pom-pom cheerleading smile. Just a simple grin. As I do, I notice that people around me smile, too. It's awesome to see that. Give it a try — share a subtle grin and see the neat responses you get. Research shows that smiling has health benefits by reducing stress, and it's contagious.

bee prepared for opportunity

All bee colonies get a new queen bee at some point, and a process of replacement begins. The bees work together to replace the queen, and it's a brutal, yet captivating process. The potential queen bees are served a special diet of "royal jelly" to help with their superior growth. Like a competing queen bee, if you want that opportunity, you must get nourished and fight for it to the end. This can be compared to succession planning in an organization. It's a talent management process used to develop and groom new potential leaders. It's also designed to maintain top talent within; those who possess valuable experience, knowledge and know-how of a company and its clients. Every company has some form of succession planning process. If you want people to know your high potential, you need to take an active role in that process. One way to get on people's radar screen is to be a high contributor and always perform at your best. Be a person who brings a great deal of value and ideas and solves problems. Some people deliberately fly low, below the flower bud, so to speak, where the radar can't see them. That's a disaster waiting to happen, in my opinion. We as humans have much more to offer.

a. succession planning is a working partnership between managers and employees

b. understand the organization's expectations and how they define high-potential employees, so you can prepare

c. It's best to begin early and not wait for a position to open — be proactive and ask questions

bee colorful

I was born with something rare called complete heterochromia, where my irises (the colored part of the eye) are different colors; one color from my mom's eyes and one from my dad's eyes. Since studying design, I've always had a fascination with color theory. Research shows that bees have favorite colors, too. You may have noticed a bee buzzing around your bright colored shirt from time to time, as it has mistaken you for a flower. Your colorful shirt was sort of attractive and expressive. We can be expressive toward others with our words as well. Have you ever heard the term, "Facts tell, stories sell?" Get away from the same old black and white fact telling and try adding some color to your communication through a story. You don't need to become a bright bulb in a dark room. You can be subtle like a dimly lit candle in a dark room and be equally effective. In fact, candlelight is natural. It's also enchanting. Who doesn't like some enchantment? Watch *The Wizard of Oz* in black and white, then again in color to see the difference color can make as it relates to impact and imagination.

worker bee or "workabee"

In a honey bee colony, a worker bee takes on different roles in the family. They are focused in the collection of food, they maintain the hive, and cooperate with one other. It's a true team effort.

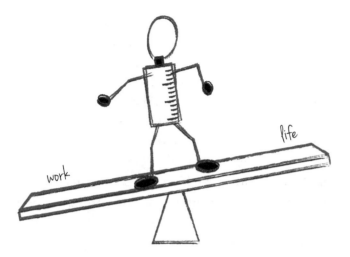

In our world, a "workabee" is known to spend too much time working and too little time at home. It's a recipe for disaster when it comes to relationships, especially your most prized ones.

Which are you? Are you a worker bee or a "workabee?"

I was once told while worker bees forage, they are known to return home at faster speeds than they departed. Their main objective is to take care of the family.

Nature is fascinating.

make lots of honey

The benefits of making GOLD are huge and require everyone on the team to play a role. Think about this. Lots of animals actually touch the beautiful flower, but the honey bee is the only creature on earth that takes the stuff and makes the honey. We know that honey is made by bees from their internal digestion and regurgitation.

The last two questions I have are:

1. What "stuff" are you digesting and regurgitating?
2. Is it making you honey or is it making you sick and tired?

Sometimes it's best to let go of the parts in your life that are not working so you can enjoy your honey.

life is golden and sweet with the right buzz

Don't close this book in the same shape you opened it. It's time to lay the cobblestone and pave the way, so let's bring this full circle. Integrating creativity and analysis is the cornerstone for CINCHOLOGY®. Add a capstone to your personal and professional building blocks in CINCH fashion by subscribing to my website and participating in a foundational or advanced webinar or seminar. Let me help you add some color and balance to your respective building blocks. The potential is endless with CINCHOLOGY®: Achieving BIG Breakthroughs One Inch at a Time.

You can find me at www.cinch-ology.com and follow me at Twitter.com/cinchology.

Let the co-creating begin! Inch-by-inch, anything's a cinch!

www.cinch-ology.com | cinchologyseries.com

CINCHOLOGIST™

I am a **CINCH**ologist™

I am known for making things easy, not difficult.

I have a blessed family and a blessed career.

I start my day with gratitude and build people up.

I am fearless because I know I'm only one simple idea away.

I am effective and confident.

I understand the powerful law of attraction.

I connect daily with something greater than myself.

I always leave a place better than the way I found it.

I am unstoppable.

I am a co-creator.

I know inch-by-inch, anything is a CINCH.

I am a **CINCH**ologist™

*"My meaning simply is, that whatever I have tried
to do in life, I have tried with all my heart to do
well; that whatever I have devoted myself to, I have
devoted myself to completely; that in great aims and in
small, I have always been thoroughly in earnest."*
– **Charles Dickens,** *David Copperfield*

BIBLIOGRAPHY

1. https://www.stress.org/stress-research/
2. Stress, Portrait of a Killer – A National Geographic Special. Dir. John Heminway 2008. Documentary.
3. Banschick M.D., M. (2012). The High Failure Rate of Second and Third Marriages. Psychology Today. Retrieved 2017-5-24. https://www.psychologytoday.com/blog/the-intelligent-divorce/201202/the-high-failure-rate-second-and-third-marriages
4. Department of Economics, Center for Neuropolicy, Emory University, Atlanta, Georgia.
5. Goizueta Business School, Emory University, Atlanta, Georgia.
6. Galaxy Stress Research, Mindlab International, Sussex University (2009) http://www.telegraph.co.uk/news/health/news/5070874/Reading-can-help-reduce-stress.html
7. Journal of the American Veterinary Medical Association. Schaumburg, Illinois, U.S.: American Veterinary Medical Association. 2000-11-01. Retrieved 2017-5-23.
8. *The neural mechanisms of learning from competitors*: Paul Howard-Jones1, Rafal Bogacz2, Jee H. Yoo2, Ute Leonards3 and Skevi Demetriou1, *NeuroImage*,

Volume 53, issue 2, pages 790-799, published November 1, 2010.

9. Fridkin, S. et al. (2014) CDC Vital Signs: Improving Antibiotic Use Among Hospitalized Patients. https://www.cdc.gov/mmwr/preview/mmwrhtml/mm6309a4.htm

10. Zimlichman E, Henderson D, Tamir O, Franz C, Song P, Yamin CK, Keohane C, Denham CR, Bates DW. Health Care–Associated Infections A Meta-analysis of Costs and Financial Impact on the US Health Care System. *JAMA Intern Med.* 2013;173(22):2039-2046. doi:10.1001/jamainternmed.2013.9763

ABOUT THE AUTHOR

Robert Louis Poole exemplifies serving. He's a U.S. Navy veteran and a highly accomplished business professional receiving numerous achievement awards and recognition from corporations like Smiths Medical, Medtronic, Kimberly-Clark and 3M. He also co-founded three small business. In addition, he served his community as a volunteer firefighter and EMT-defibrillation. Robert is consultant, speaker and a contributor of published articles in community and local papers. Although a New Yorker by heart, he resides in the beautiful foothills of North Carolina with his wife, two daughters and their four pampered pooches. You can find him at www.cinch-ology.com and follow him at twitter.com/cinchology

DISCARD

CPSIA information can be obtained
at www.ICGtesting.com
Printed in the USA
BVHW07s1337300918
528864BV00002B/6/P